THE BEDFORD SERIES IN HISTORY AND CULTURE

The Mexican Revolution

A Brief History with Documents

Related Titles in
THE BEDFORD SERIES IN HISTORY AND CULTURE

Advisory Editors: Lynn Hunt, *University of California, Los Angeles*
David W. Blight, *Yale University*
Bonnie G. Smith, *Rutgers University*
Natalie Zemon Davis, *Princeton University*
Ernest R. May, *Harvard University*

Victors and Vanquished: Spanish and Nahua Views of the Conquest of Mexico
Edited with an Introduction by Stuart B. Schwartz, *Yale University*

The French Revolution and Human Rights: A Brief Documentary History
Edited, Translated, and with an Introduction by Lynn Hunt, *University of California, Los Angeles*

Slave Revolution in the Caribbean, 1789–1804: A Brief History with Documents
Laurent Dubois, *Michigan State University*, and John D. Garrigus, *Jacksonville University*

The U.S. War with Mexico: A Brief History with Documents
Ernesto Chávez, *University of Texas at El Paso*

Talking Back to Civilization: Indian Voices from the Progressive Era
Edited with an Introduction by Frederick E. Hoxie, *University of Illinois at Urbana–Champaign*

Lenin and the Making of the Soviet State: A Brief History with Documents
Jeffrey Brooks, *Johns Hopkins University*, and Georgiy Chernyavskiy, *Ukrainian Academy of Culture*

Mao Zedong and China's Revolutions: A Brief History with Documents
Timothy Cheek, *University of British Columbia*

The First World War: A Brief History with Documents
Susan R. Grayzel, *University of Mississippi*

July 1914: Soldiers, Statesmen, and the Coming of the Great War: A Brief Documentary History
Samuel R. Williamson Jr., *University of the South*, and Russel Van Wyk, *University of North Carolina at Chapel Hill*

César Chávez: A Brief Biography with Documents
Edited with an Introduction by Richard W. Etulain, *University of New Mexico*

THE BEDFORD SERIES IN HISTORY AND CULTURE

The Mexican Revolution
A Brief History with Documents

Mark Wasserman
Rutgers University

BEDFORD / ST. MARTIN'S   Boston ◆ New York

For Bedford/St. Martin's

Publisher for History: Mary V. Dougherty
Director of Development for History: Jane Knetzger
Senior Editor: Heidi L. Hood
Developmental Editor: Dean DeChambeau
Associate Editor: Jennifer Jovin
Editorial Assistant: Laura Kintz
Production Supervisor: Dennis J. Conroy
Executive Marketing Manager: Jenna Bookin Barry
Project Management: Books By Design, Inc.
Cartography: Mapping Specialists, Ltd.
Text Design: Claire Seng-Niemoeller
Cover Design: Marine Miller
Cover Photo: Mexican Revolutionaries. Two revolutionary couples photographed
 ca. 1910. Image No. 0048697. The Granger Collection, NYC—All rights reserved.
Composition: Achorn International, Inc.
Printing and Binding: RR Donnelley and Sons

President: Joan E. Feinberg
Editorial Director: Denise B. Wydra
Director of Marketing: Karen R. Soeltz
Director of Production: Susan W. Brown
Associate Director, Editorial Production: Elise S. Kaiser
Manager, Publishing Services: Andrea Cava

Library of Congress Control Number: 2011944989

For information, write: Bedford/St. Martin's, 75 Arlington Street, Boston, MA 02116
(617-399-4000)

ISBN: 978-0-312-53504-9

Acknowledgments

Acknowledgments and copyrights are continued at the back of the book on page 159, which constitutes an extension of the copyright page.

Distributed outside North America by PALGRAVE MACMILLAN
Houndmills, Basingstoke, Hampshire RG21 6XS

To my teachers,
John J. TePaske, John Tate Lanning,
John H. Coatsworth, and Friedrich Katz,
and my colleague Samuel L. Bailey

Foreword

The Bedford Series in History and Culture is designed so that readers can study the past as historians do.

The historian's first task is finding the evidence. Documents, letters, memoirs, interviews, pictures, movies, novels, or poems can provide facts and clues. Then the historian questions and compares the sources. There is more to do than in a courtroom, for hearsay evidence is welcome, and the historian is usually looking for answers beyond act and motive. Different views of an event may be as important as a single verdict. How a story is told may yield as much information as what it says.

Along the way the historian seeks help from other historians and perhaps from specialists in other disciplines. Finally, it is time to write, to decide on an interpretation and how to arrange the evidence for readers.

Each book in this series contains an important historical document or group of documents, each document a witness from the past and open to interpretation in different ways. The documents are combined with some element of historical narrative—an introduction or a biographical essay, for example—that provides students with an analysis of the primary source material and important background information about the world in which it was produced.

Each book in the series focuses on a specific topic within a specific historical period. Each provides a basis for lively thought and discussion about several aspects of the topic and the historian's role. Each is short enough (and inexpensive enough) to be a reasonable one-week assignment in a college course. Whether as classroom or personal reading, each book in the series provides firsthand experience of the challenge—and fun—of discovering, recreating, and interpreting the past.

Lynn Hunt
David W. Blight
Bonnie G. Smith
Natalie Zemon Davis
Ernest R. May

Preface

The Mexican Revolution is one of the three epic stories of Mexican history, the other two being the encounter between Europeans and indigenous peoples in the sixteenth century and the decade-long war of independence in the nineteenth century. All were complex events that involved brutal, prolonged violence and featured larger-than-life figures as well as people from multiple walks of life. Our knowledge of these watersheds has changed greatly over the past half-century as new evidence has come to light. We have reread and reinterpreted existing documentation; discovered new materials once hidden in dusty, dark rooms; opened new archives; interviewed elderly people; and employed new techniques borrowed from other disciplines.

During and in the wake of the events that took place in Mexico from 1910 to 1940, historians and artists regarded the Revolution as a people's movement, whose greatest heroes had championed the just redistribution of land (Emiliano Zapata and Lázaro Cárdenas) or equal access to government (Francisco I. Madero). The great muralist painters of the 1920s and 1930s—Diego Rivera, David Siqueiros, and José Orozco—glorified the Revolution's achievements on behalf of the peasants and workers. Only a few novelists, such as Mariano Azuela in *The Underdogs* and Martín Luis Guzmán in *The Eagle and the Serpent*, dissented from that positive view.

Perceptions changed during the 1960s, when historians began to revise their assessments. A far more cynical interpretation of the Revolution predominated for the next four decades. The Revolution, the revisionists claimed, had not been a people's movement, but rather a reinvention of corrupt dictatorship. Reform, they maintained, had been a fraud. In recent times, mostly because of extensive research in state and municipal archives throughout Mexico, a more balanced view has emerged. On one hand, we have found that in both the countryside and the cities, peasants and workers participated in and shaped the events of the Revolution. They also won some hard-fought victories.

Zapata's followers, for example, instituted land reform, destroying the sugar planter class that had oppressed the people of Morelos during the decades before the Revolution. On the other hand, we have discovered that much of the land reform accomplished was political—the revolutionary government redistributed land in return for support. The same was true for the gains obtained by labor unions. Only those who cooperated with the revolutionary regime received the benefits of reform. Thus, reform became not the result of social justice, but a political payoff. This volume aims to make these nuances of the Revolution accessible to students.

The introduction and documents that follow try to present the middle ground between these two disparate views of the Revolution. They portray the upheaval as simultaneously based on widespread popular support and participation and manipulated by the elites. There was plenty of corruption throughout, but there were also substantial gains by the people. There was brutality and idealism, treachery and stubborn loyalty. The leaders of the Revolution were both heroes and villains. This volume tries to balance the "high" politics of the proclamations, decrees, and laws with the "low" politics of the people.

Part one, the introduction, supplies a contextual overview of the Revolution. It sets out the broad narrative of the history of Mexico, beginning with the nation's independence and continuing through the difficult nineteenth century, when ongoing war stunted economic growth and profound disagreements tainted politics. It then explores the era of the dictator Porfirio Díaz, who established a measure of order and progress by means of a changing set of extraordinary arrangements, achieved through both negotiation and coercion. Finally, the introduction examines the complex politics and brutal military conflicts of the Revolution itself. It outlines the multifaceted nature of the conflict and the many movements—led by different people, propounding particular ideologies, and taking place in various localities—within the larger historical event.

Part one first explores the events, developments, and processes that led to the discontent that made the Revolution possible, then analyzes the immediate causes of the political and social eruption that occurred in 1910. The most violent phase of the Revolution takes up most of the narrative, with an emphasis on the brutality of the conflict, the actions of its leaders, and, most important, the lives of the soldiers and civilians who endured the suffering and losses. The introduction also devotes attention to the actions of military and civilian women, whom past historians have often left out. Women participated in battles, acted as labor organizers, sought the return of village land, and fought for equal rights in the workplace and the voting booth. Following this discussion, the introduction turns to the results of the Revolution. Here the concentration is on the radical nature of the transformations authorized by the Constitution of 1917 and on the differences between the law as laid out in the constitution and the actuality of reform. Lastly, the narrative explores the international aspects of the Revolution, including the involvement of foreign investors, the invasions by the United States, and the diplomatic machinations of the great European powers.

In the first section of part two, the documents were selected to illuminate the process by which Mexicans of all classes made the profound decision to rebel against firmly entrenched authority and risk their lives for their cause. Getting inside the minds of turn-of-the-twentieth-century peasants, workers, middle-class people, and wealthy elites is, of course, virtually impossible. We have to rely on the words of rabble-rousers such as the Flores Magón brothers, who founded the Mexican Liberal party; the wealthy landowner Francisco I. Madero; the agents of Emiliano Zapata who wrote his proclamations; or even middle-class novelists to present us with clues.

In the next three sections of part two, we get a more direct glimpse of the hardships and inequities suffered by everyday people through their own eyes, including photographs and written accounts. These selections provide poignant pictures of the battlefield from the memoirs of generals, other veterans, and foreigners. Veterans' organizations, oral history projects, and family historians have gathered the remembrances of some of the people who fought and endured. In their own words, these Mexicans, who survived both the war and the peace, describe their lives.

In the concluding sections of part two, we gain insight into the political aspects of the Revolution. I have tried to put forth a balanced view, including the reminiscences of winners and losers. I also present official documents, such as the Constitution of 1917 and reports of government investigations, to assess the Revolution's accomplishments and explore its international ramifications.

Several pedagogical aids support students' synthesis of the material in this volume. A map of Mexico in 1910 orients students to the geography of the Revolution. A chronology charts important events. Questions for consideration ask students to think critically about the documents. Finally, the selected bibliography contains numerous sources for further research.

A NOTE ABOUT THE DOCUMENTS

Most of the sources in this collection come from the personal remembrances of the participants, including well-known and everyday people,
Mexicans as well as foreigners. These sources all present challenges in
their reliability. The high-profile people, of course, had the not-so-hidden
goal of making themselves look better. Their memoirs were, to our benefit, for the most part written soon after or during the events described.
The peasants and workers, while undoubtedly also seeking to present
themselves in a good light, did not speak about their memories until
approached by scholars decades after the events. There are clearly difficulties in using any of these memoirs without scrutiny. Beyond these
sources, the options are limited. Other observations come from foreigners living in Mexico who served as diplomats, journalists, or businesspeople. But foreigners were often biased sources. The Revolution took
place during an age in which racism dominated. Prejudiced foreigners
were often condescending toward Mexicans. We must interpret their
observations carefully. Even official documents must be regarded with
a sharp eye. Nonetheless, when examined closely, with an awareness of
their shortcomings, the sources presented provide an evocative view of
the Revolution.

ACKNOWLEDGMENTS

Many thanks to Paul Hart, Gilbert Joseph, Allen Wells, Anne Ruben-
stein, Friedrich Katz, Julia Swanson, and Glen Kuecker for providing me
with good suggestions and actual documents. I am indebted to several
people who provided useful feedback on the first draft of this book: Dale
Graden, University of Idaho; Paul Hart, Texas State University–San
Marcos; Susie Porter, University of Utah; Stephanie Smith, Ohio State
University; Doug Tompson, Columbus (Georgia) State University; Evan
Ward, Brigham Young University; and Thomas Whigham, University
of Georgia. I would also like to express my gratitude to Dean DeCham-
beau for his very helpful developmental editing. Thanks as well to Mary
Dougherty and Heidi Hood at Bedford/St. Martin's for their assistance.
My final thanks go to Bonnie Smith for suggesting the project.

                                                        Mark Wasserman

Contents

APPENDIXES

Illustrations

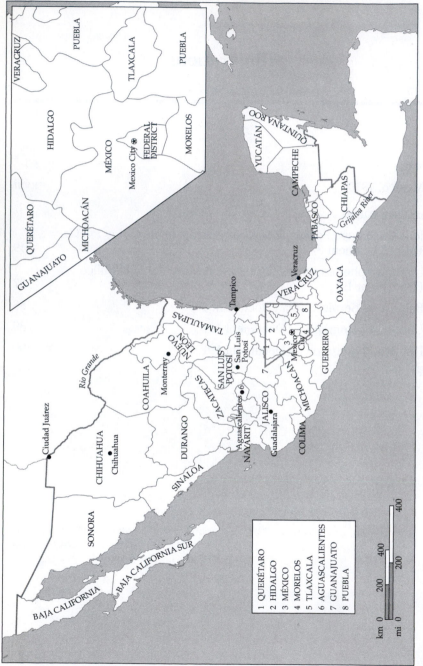

Mexico, 1910

1 QUERÉTARO
2 HIDALGO
3 MÉXICO
4 MORELOS
5 TLAXCALA
6 AGUASCALIENTES
7 GUANAJUATO
8 PUEBLA

PART ONE

Introduction:
The Causes, Course, and
Consequences of the
Mexican Revolution

The Mexican Revolution (1910–1920) was, with the Chinese and Russian revolutions (1911 and 1917, respectively), the first of the epic revolutions of the twentieth century. Lasting more than a decade, it cost the lives of between one million and two million Mexicans and caused widespread damage. As a result of the destruction and disruptions of war, the Mexican economy did not return to its prerevolution levels for perhaps two decades. The Revolution also produced the most radical constitution written anywhere in the world up to that time, the Constitution of 1917.

The Mexican Revolution stands out among other twentieth-century revolutions in a number of ways. First, unlike the revolutions in China, Russia, Cuba, Vietnam, and Nicaragua, it was not based on communist ideology. Although its leaders advocated land reform and later redistributed massive amounts of land to nearly two million peasants, the new regime did not renounce capitalism or institute a socialist state. Also unlike the Soviet Union (Stalin) and China (Mao), the Mexican Revolution did not lead to a prolonged, bloody dictatorship. Instead, a one-party state emerged and endured for seventy years.

In addition, at a time when the emerging middle class and urban industrial workers and elites throughout Latin America sought (and sometimes fought for) the right to share more fairly in politics and economic development, only in Mexico did small landowners, landless peasants, factory workers, miners, members of the middle class (government bureaucrats, small-business owners, small-scale merchants), and dissident elites form a multiclass alliance that overthrew an existing regime dominated by a small ruling class. Elsewhere in Latin America, in almost every instance, the middle class allied with the upper class and military to suppress rural and urban workers and peasants.

The Mexican Revolution also stands out because it succeeded despite the heavy involvement of the United States, which invaded Mexico twice during these years (in 1914 and 1916) and steadfastly opposed reform efforts that might have adversely affected American investments. In addition, because the Revolution partially coincided with World War I, it had a broad international scope, involving several of the Great Powers. Germany's efforts in 1916 and 1917 to persuade the new revolutionary government, headed by Venustiano Carranza, to enter the war on its side in great measure precipitated the United States' entry into the war. Finally, the Mexican Revolution influenced Latin Americans by sending a stark warning to the hemisphere's ruling classes that they would have to confront growing demands for political and economic equality and social justice from the middle and working classes.

THE BACKGROUND OF THE REVOLUTION

The Mexican Revolution resulted from historical processes that can be traced back to the interactions of Europeans and indigenous peoples during the Spanish conquest of the sixteenth century. These processes spanned three hundred years of Spanish colonial rule and decades of troubled politics and economics after Mexicans won their independence from Spain in 1821.

The first half-century after Mexico declared its independence in 1810 brought nearly ceaseless foreign wars and civil strife. The war of independence lasted for more than a decade and took a heavy toll. It ruined the economy, especially its core industry, mining. The second pillar of the economy, the great landed estates known as *haciendas*, deteriorated badly as well. A long series of foreign invasions and internal conflicts exacerbated economic conditions, eating up whatever scarce human and material resources were available.

In 1829, Spain briefly and unsuccessfully attempted to reconquer its former colony. Seven years later, in 1836, the far northern province of

Texas rebelled against the central government and won its independence. In 1838, France staged a short-lived invasion, supposedly to
collect damages owed its citizens, which they had incurred in earlier
upheavals in Mexico. The worst was yet to come, however. In 1846,
the United States provoked a war with Mexico in order to defend its
annexation of Texas the year before and to acquire the territory that
now includes the states of California, Arizona, New Mexico, Utah, and
part of Oklahoma. Two years later, Mexico suffered a crushing defeat
and lost half its national territory. Antonio López de Santa Anna, the
nation's best military leader, dominated politics from 1821 to 1855. He
led the nation to its victories over Spain and France, but also to its costly
defeats to Texas and the United States.

From 1857 to 1860, Mexico endured a bloody civil war. Known as
the War of the Reform, it was fought by two rival political factions—the
Conservatives, who favored a centralized government and supported
the Roman Catholic Church, and the Liberals, who advocated local and
state autonomy and opposed the church and were against collective landholding in Indian villages. No sooner had that war ended than in 1861 a
brief alliance of Britain, Spain, and France invaded Veracruz, Mexico's
major port on the Gulf of Mexico, in an effort to force Mexico to repay
its debts to European lenders. Britain and Spain quickly withdrew their
forces, but France remained, conquering almost all of the country and
installing the archduke of Austria, Maximilian, as emperor. (This became
known as the French Intervention.) The Mexicans, led by President
Benito Juárez, defeated Maximilian in 1867. Brave and stubborn beyond
measure, Juárez survived exile, personal tragedies, and a series of
military defeats at the hands of the French to overcome the invaders.
Another decade of revolts and uncertainty followed. With the advent of
the dictatorship of General Porfirio Díaz, Mexico finally experienced a
prolonged period of peace (1877–1910).

The crucial political issue of the era from independence into the
twentieth century was the extent of local and state autonomy. Beginning
with Juárez, Liberals, its advocates, came to the realization that local
autonomy would not allow Mexicans to formulate a national identity or
to construct a modern, capitalist economy. As a result, Juárez—and
later Díaz, also a Liberal—created a stronger federal government.

Porfirio Díaz, from the southern state of Oaxaca, gained prominence
as a young military officer during the French Intervention. He was one
of the heroes of the battle of Cinco de Mayo (May 5, 1862), when the
Mexican army defeated (temporarily) the invading French forces at
Puebla, on the route between Veracruz and Mexico City. By the late

1860s, as part of a generation of precocious and ambitious Liberals, Díaz regarded Juárez as someone whose time had passed. He led a rebellion against Juárez in 1872 and suffered a humiliating defeat. Nonetheless, he recovered to try again in 1876, overthrowing Juárez's successor, Sebastián Lerdo de Tejada. Díaz ruled until 1880, when he voluntarily ceded the presidency to Manuel González, a close ally. Díaz returned to office by election in 1884 and remained there until 1911.

Díaz proved a brilliant politician, ruling adeptly with a mixture of political negotiations and selective, if at times brutal, coercion. Over thirty-five years, he constructed a political economy based on expanding exports of minerals and agricultural commodities (cattle and henequen, the fiber from a species of agave that could be made into twine), foreign investment, and improved transportation. He put together an intricate mosaic of arrangements with local and regional elites that limited the impact of the regionalism that had dominated Mexican history since independence. Díaz astutely mollified his opposition by allowing them to become rich. By the time of his last reelection in 1910, he had a worldwide reputation as a powerful leader, and Mexico had achieved a considerable measure of order and progress. Díaz's policies produced economic growth and modernization, but although conditions for many people improved from the late 1890s through 1907, prosperity was unequally shared, leaving out most of the working people in rural areas and the cities. Perhaps more important, his rule never completely eliminated the local and regional orientation of politics. The issues of economic inequity and local autonomy fueled the revolution that erupted in 1910.

THE ORIGINS OF THE REVOLUTION

Three immediate crises precipitated the Mexican Revolution: the economic depression of 1907–1909, the eruption of rural unrest, and the political succession to Díaz. The most important was the depression, which undermined Díaz's support among the upper classes. His web of political alliances depended on his ability to reward cooperation with jobs, tax exemptions, subsidies for businesses, and other benefits. But he could not pay for cooperation unless the economy flourished. With resources scarce, regional groups bought off by Díaz bickered more intensely. Old wounds were rubbed raw. At the same time, the economic downturn ruined the emerging middle class. Many businesses built by the middle class during the previous decade went bankrupt and the expansion of new businesses halted abruptly. All the unfairness of the regime, under which the middle class suffered discrimination in taxation, the courts, and the banking system, was laid bare in the depression. The working class, particularly in the mining regions, was also adversely affected, as the depression caused widespread unemployment. Many of those who kept their jobs had to accept lower wages and reduced working hours.

At the same time, the countryside had reached the point of rebellion. Improved transportation and larger markets for agricultural commodities both in Mexico and abroad had driven up land values, causing political officials and large landowners to expand their landholdings. In order to satisfy the demand for export commodities, they had expropriated the property of small landowners and the communally held land of Indian villages. The displaced farmers were driven into a pool of cheap, landless labor. The crisis intensified in 1907 when the economic downturn eliminated alternative employment opportunities for landless people in the mines, the cities, and the United States. To make matters worse, many workers returned to their villages from the cities and across the border, increasing the pressures on already minimal resources. Because the large estate owners and politicians had taken their land, villagers were unable to grow enough food to feed themselves.

Country people also were discontented about the loss of local autonomy. The Díaz dictatorship had eliminated elections to local offices and instead installed appointed district bosses, who often proved unresponsive and oppressive. These government agents, in many cases people from outside the area, trampled local customs and traditions. But the rural population was not about to rebel unless there was at least some chance of achieving positive results. A split among the ruling elites gave them an opportunity.

The third and most immediate crisis—the furor over succession—led to critical divisions within the political elite. Seventy-four years old when reelected in 1904, Díaz committed the fundamental mistake of many dictators: He refused to provide for a peaceful succession after his retirement or death. More egregiously, Díaz offered to retire but then reneged, creating a political crisis. In an interview with an American journalist named James Creelman in 1908 (Document 2), Díaz bragged that Mexico was ready for democracy and that he would step down in 1910. He professed that he welcomed political competition. When news of the interview hit the streets of Mexico City, politicians were puzzled and afraid. They suspected the wily old dictator was trying to flush out overambitious or disloyal allies. Díaz quickly changed his mind and announced for reelection, but he had shaken the status quo.

Within the regime, two major factions warily eyed each other as Díaz aged. On one side were the old generals, some of whom had risen with the dictator. They were veterans of the Indian wars of the last quarter of the nineteenth century against the Yaquis in the north and the Mayas in the south. The leader of this group was General Bernardo Reyes, the military zone commander and political boss of Nuevo León, in northeastern Mexico. He had very loyal followers and important ties to the state's industrialists based in Monterrey. Many of the discontented looked to Reyes for leadership. Díaz reacted by sending the general to Europe on an inconsequential diplomatic mission in the fall of 1908. This left his faction without a leader, at least temporarily.

On the other side were the *científicos*, a small circle of highly placed technocrats led by Díaz's finance minister, José Yves Limantour. The *científicos* adhered to the positivist philosophy, placing their trust in science and progress. They were the strongest advocates of Mexican modernization. Limantour, however, was ineligible to succeed Díaz because his father was French. The *científicos* had grown impatient with Díaz in the years before 1910 because the dictator had seemed to step back from his earlier support of their economic policies.

In addition to the division within the political elite and his alienation of a good number of formerly loyal adherents, there is evidence that Díaz had alienated some of the large foreign interests that had helped him ascend to power and had fueled the engine of Mexican economic development. Díaz had taken a number of measures to limit the influence of foreign corporations, including the nationalization of the railroad system between 1902 and 1911. In particular, after 1900 Díaz had sought to balance U.S. and European interests—most notably in the petroleum industry—to maintain his own stature and Mexican sovereignty. Some historians have concluded that American petroleum companies and their affiliated New York banks sponsored the opposition to Díaz that emerged during his last two years in office.

There were early warnings that the regime was on shaky ground, including a strike by miners at the Cananea Consolidated Copper Company in Sonora in 1906, which the government repressed quickly. The Mexican Liberal party, which brought together northern middle and working class, staged brief revolts from 1906 through 1911. That previewed the vertical class alliance that in 1910 rallied around Francisco I. Madero in opposition to Díaz (Document 1).

Madero was a large landowner from the northern state of Coahuila. His family was one of the richest in Mexico and one of the regional elites pushed aside by Díaz in the 1880s. Madero unified the various discontented groups and forged them, at least temporarily, into an alliance. To the disgruntled upper class, he was one of them. To the middle class, who primarily sought to gain entry into the political process, his demand for a return to the open access to government provided in the Constitution of 1857 promised not only fairer politics but a more equitable economic system as well. And to the lower class, his relatively enlightened employment practices offered hope. In addition to his cross-class appeal, he may have appeared to some foreign interests as being more modern and perhaps more pliable than the old warhorse Díaz. Even the *científicos* may have found him an acceptable alternative to the increasingly uncooperative dictator.

In 1909, Madero took on the impossible task of challenging Díaz's reelection. The previous year, he had published a book, *The Presidential Succession of 1910*, taking Díaz to task for his harsh and unfair rule. He then embarked on an independent campaign for the presidency. Short and with a squeaky voice, Madero hardly looked or sounded the part of a charismatic leader. Nonetheless, as he traveled the nation in late 1909, he showed courage and fortitude. As the crowds grew larger and more boisterous, his Anti-Reelectionist party gained momentum. The party met in April 1910 and nominated Madero as its candidate for president. He championed democracy as the foundation of his program. Other reforms, such as the return of land taken from the villages, would follow. Feeling threatened, Díaz cracked down on the opposition, jailing Madero and winning the June election. He then released Madero, who fled across the border into the United States.

Madero reluctantly and correctly concluded that Díaz would not retire peacefully. In October, he proclaimed his Plan of San Luis Potosí (Document 3), which called for the Mexican people to follow him and restore democracy. The pronouncement also called for the restoration of land taken illegally from smallholders by the Díaz regime. Madero returned to his homeland on November 19, 1910. The Mexican Revolution had begun.

The upheaval that followed included several stages: the overthrow of Díaz (1911); the subsequent presidency of Madero (1911–1913); his overthrow by the counterrevolution led by General Victoriano Huerta (March 1913); the defeat of Huerta (1914) by a coalition of former Madero supporters; a bitter civil war between the victorious revolutionaries, led by Francisco "Pancho" Villa and Emiliano Zapata on one side and Venustiano Carranza and Alvaro Obregón on the other (1914–1917); the triumph of the least radical revolutionary faction, headed by Carranza (1917–1920); his subsequent overthrow by his best general,

Obregón (1920); a prolonged period of reconstruction under Presidents Obregón (1920–1924), Plutarco Elías Calles (1924–1928), and Calles's three short-term puppets (1928–1934); and the radical presidency of Lázaro Cárdenas (1934–1940).[1] The current volume looks at the period from 1910 to 1924.

The events of these years were further complicated because, even when united under one figure such as Madero or Carranza, the Mexican Revolution was divided into distinct geographic entities. The northern revolution consisted of small landholders, some of them Protestant converts, many of whom were also small-scale entrepreneurs, such as muleteers and storekeepers. Some of these revolutionaries, mostly from Chihuahua and Sonora, were residents of communities that had originated as *presidios*, a string of forts along the northern frontier established during colonial times to fight indigenous peoples such as the Apaches and Comanches. They were veterans of the long wars with the Indians, which had ended only in the mid-1890s, and were used to their autonomy. In Chihuahua, for seven decades after independence, they had fought in alliance with local hacienda owners for their own peace and prosperity without much help from Mexico City. But the Díaz regime had encroached on their prerogatives and traditions, stolen their land, and taken away their self-rule. These northerners were armed and mobile, and they were formidable foes.

The Sonorans, led by Obregón and Calles, were latecomers who joined the Revolution during the Madero presidency. They came from a less rough-and-tumble environment than the Chihuahuan presidio dwellers. The Sonorans firmly believed in capitalism and private property. They were not enthusiastic about redistributing land to the landless.

The southern revolutionaries were composed of villagers who had lost their land to the great haciendas. The core of the southern uprising was in Morelos, a state immediately south of the capital, where the sugar haciendas had pushed aside the old collective communities. Other villagers from the states of Puebla, Guerrero, Tlaxcala, and Oaxaca also fought for land reform. These small farmers from the south, like their brethren in the north, sought not only to restore their land and thus obtain land for the landless but also to reconstitute their control over their everyday lives. In part, theirs was a movement to win back local autonomy. Northern and southern revolutionaries had these goals in common, but they differed sharply in that a less radical, more politically oriented middle-class outlook predominated among northerners.

Underlying the dissidence that arose from the inequities of land-ownership in the countryside was race. Rural people fell mostly into one of two categories: Indians, descendants of the original peoples of Mexico whom the Europeans had met at the time of the conquest in the sixteenth century; and mestizos and mulattoes, or mixed bloods, the products of miscegenation between Indians and Europeans and between Africans and Europeans, respectively.[2] The villages that were often at the center of revolutionary discontent also varied in the racial composition of their residents, with some entirely Indian, others mes-tizo, and still others with Indians and mestizos (or mulattoes in some areas such as the state of Guerrero). Indian villagers maintained their own customs, often did not speak Spanish, and through much of the nineteenth century governed themselves. There were frequently hard feelings between Indians and mestizos, with the former claiming that the latter sought to exploit them. In the far north in Sonora and in the far south in Yucatán, the indigenous peoples fought fiercely to keep their land and their autonomy. The Yaquis of Sonora fought the Díaz administration in a series of bitter wars. The Mayas of Yucatán nearly pushed whites and mestizos from their region in the 1840s and main-tained considerable independence throughout the Díaz era in the region of Quintana Roo. The Yaquis, Mayas, and other Indian peoples suffered badly from discrimination and persecution by whites and mestizos, who wanted their land and labor while disdaining their cultures. The elites during the Díaz era were particularly oppressive, for their leaders saw indigenous peoples as impediments to the progress of the nation. Indi-ans played an important role militarily in parts of Mexico during the Revolution, in particular the Yaquis in Sonora, who fought on the side of the Constitutionalists led by Obregón. Many revolutionaries sought to incorporate indigenous peoples into modern society through education. Others, such as the artist Diego Rivera, glorified Mexico's Indian past, especially the accomplishments of the Aztecs.

The Revolution began in the northern state of Chihuahua on Novem-ber 20, 1910, when Madero proclaimed his Plan of San Luis Potosí. Small landholders from villages in western Chihuahua under the leadership of Pascual Orozco, a muleteer and merchant, recognized Madero as their leader and conducted a guerrilla war against the federal army. Madero, returning to Mexico after his brief exile in the United States, joined the rebels, who continued to wage their campaign through the spring of 1911, when they lay siege to the border town of Ciudad Juárez (just across from El Paso, Texas). In early May, Orozco and his underling

Francisco "Pancho" Villa forced the federal garrison to surrender. By then, rebels had risen all over the country, and the federal army was unable to restore order.

Díaz had purposely allowed the army to deteriorate to prevent potential revolts against his regime. Its officer corps was aged and infirm. It was said that some of them could barely mount their horses. Many of the generals were corrupt, collecting the pay of nonexistent soldiers. The president periodically shifted his zone commanders so that they could not build power bases that might challenge his authority. When met by a determined opposition in more than one region, the army proved incapable of defeating the guerrillas.

Díaz, recognizing that his support among the elite had eroded badly and his army was in shambles, went into exile in May 1911. He might also have been worried about a U.S. invasion, as President William Howard Taft had ordered a large contingent of troops to the border area. After negotiations with the rebels, Díaz left the nation under the rule of an interim government headed by Francisco León de la Barra, a longtime official in the Díaz regime. The old army and bureaucracy remained intact. The rebels were to disarm. Meanwhile, the nation would hold a new presidential election. The brief and nearly bloodless rebellion had ended with an improbable victory.

VICTORY, COUNTERREVOLUTION, AND CIVIL WAR

Almost immediately, the cross-class coalition fell apart. The groups that had allied to oust Díaz quickly disagreed about the pace and extent of reforms, and fighting resumed. The crucial conflict occurred in the countryside. In Morelos, for example, Emiliano Zapata had successfully fought the Díaz army under the slogan "Land and Liberty." His followers, known as Zapatistas, believed that the authorities and the owners of large estates had unjustly stolen their land, and now they wanted it back. But to return their property, the government would have to expropriate it from politically well-connected large landowners. Newly elected President Madero instead called for due process. He maintained that the courts or the congress would decide on the redistribution of land after pondering the issue. When the impatient Zapatistas demanded immediate restitution and refused to put down their arms, Madero faced open rebellion.

Additional conflicts of interest arose. Miners and other industrial workers sought higher wages and improved working conditions. For workers to obtain these goals, mine and textile plant owners would have to make unwanted concessions. Some of these businesspeople had supported Madero or had close connections to his family. The middle class, too, valued the rights of private property, in direct contradiction to the demands of workers and landless country people.

After Madero took office in November 1911, he was unable to satisfy his lower-class allies. He faced an angry Pascual Orozco, who felt shunted aside even though he had won the major battle of the Revolution. Madero had insisted that a civilian become governor of Chihuahua rather than Orozco, who was insulted by his appointment as state chief of police. Orozco was a dangerous foe. The Zapatistas, as we have already seen, also refused to lay down their arms. Thus, Madero faced open opposition in both the north (Orozco) and the south (the Zapatistas). In the meantime, two factions of the old regime took up arms. General Bernardo Reyes at last moved into active opposition to Madero. And the former dictator's nephew, Félix Díaz, claimed his right to succeed his uncle.

Madero and his revolutionary allies, together with the old federal army headed by General Victoriano Huerta, defeated Orozco in a series of bloody battles in the north in the summer of 1912. Zapata's guerrillas remained in the field, however. In February 1913, Reyes and Díaz joined forces and staged a revolt in Mexico City. The heavy fighting in the capital, which came to be known as the Ten Tragic Days, resulted almost immediately in Reyes's death. The contending forces then became locked in a bloody stalemate. At that point, Huerta betrayed Madero. He made Madero resign at gunpoint and then had him assassinated. The most vicious and costly phase of the Revolution—the counterrevolution—had begun.

As Huerta sought to return to the Díaz system of government, several regional revolutionary bosses resisted the new regime. The most prominent of these was Venustiano Carranza, the governor of the northern state of Coahuila. Carranza had two key generals, Pancho Villa from Chihuahua, who led a brilliant campaign against Huerta, and Alvaro Obregón from Sonora. Their movement became known as the Constitutionalists (because they wanted to reestablish the liberal principles of the Constitution of 1857). The United States aided their efforts in 1914 by occupying the country's two major ports on the Gulf of Mexico, Tampico and Veracruz, effectively cutting off Huerta's arms supply and his government's most important revenue source, customs receipts. Allied loosely with Zapata, the Constitutionalists defeated Huerta the same year.

The country was then plunged into a civil war between two factions of the victorious revolutionaries, the Conventionalists (Villa and Zapata) and the Constitutionalists (Carranza and Obregón). The Conventionalists sought more radical, immediate reforms, confiscating large estates in Zapata's territory and redistributing the land to the villagers. The Constitutionalists resisted land reform. In a series of brutal battles in north-central Mexico in 1915, Obregón and Carranza (who proclaimed himself the First Chief—chief executive—of the nation in May 1915) defeated Villa. Zapata remained peripheral to these battles. The United States recognized the Carranza government that year.

Over the next two years, Villa continued to fight a guerrilla war, precipitating a U.S. military invasion of Mexico in mid-1916 after he raided Columbus, New Mexico. Villa eventually made peace with Carranza's successor in 1920 and was killed in an ambush in Chihuahua in 1923.

Zapata withdrew to fight his own guerrilla war in his home state of Morelos and the neighboring states of Puebla and México. In 1919, Carranza had Zapata killed.

By 1917, the civil war was over. That year, Carranza was elected president, and a constitutional convention was held in Querétaro. The result, the Constitution of 1917, was a radical document that provided for the redistribution of land from wealthy owners to poor farmers and for better conditions for workers (Documents 31 and 32). Differences arose, however, over how quickly to implement the reforms and over the choice of Carranza's successor in 1920. The more reform-minded Obregón thought the new regime would have to satisfy immediately at least some of the demands of the lower classes for land redistribution and better working conditions. He also believed that he had earned the right to the presidency on the battlefield. When he rebelled, his soldiers captured and executed Carranza. Obregón then won election to the presidency in 1920.

The Constitutionalists were ultimately victorious in 1917 for several reasons: (1) they had the best general, Obregón, who adapted to modern warfare the most adeptly; (2) they had the most resources, controlling customs at the major port of Veracruz, which allowed them to purchase arms and munitions; (3) their opposition, Zapata and Villa, were unable or unwilling to coordinate their military operations; and (4) Carranza was flexible enough to win over both organized labor (in 1914) and just enough of the rebels in the villages (through his Agrarian Law of 1915; Document 26) to tip the balance of popular support in his favor.

THE HARD LIFE OF THE REVOLUTION

The impact of the revolution was widespread. Military and civilian casualties may have reached two million, and the damage to property was extensive. Soldiers lived harsh lives, with supplies often scarce, uniforms and equipment substandard, and leadership and discipline erratic. Daily life for civilians in many areas of the country also was quite dangerous. Armies came and went, taking what they needed often without consideration of the local population. Starvation was not uncommon. Extortion and taxation siphoned off any surplus capital. Although jobs were generally hard to find, some sectors had labor shortages. Transportation and communication were endlessly disrupted. Conscription and death shattered families. Some women went off to war, suffering the same hardships as men. Other women remained at home, struggling to sustain their families without their husbands. While the economy functioned, it did not grow.

The soldiers' life, in the absence of written memoirs, is difficult to re-create. Most combatants were illiterate. They were too busy trying to survive from one day to the next to bother with diaries or other such records, even if they were literate. Those who wrote their reminiscences, such as Villa, Obregón, and Marcelo Caraveo (Documents 11, 14, and 18), all generals, concentrated mostly on strategies and tactics or political maneuverings rather than on the drudgery and horror of fighting a war. Most of the fiction of the era, such as Carlos Fuentes's *The Death of Artemio Cruz* and Gregorio López y Fuentes's *El Indio* (Document 21), emphasizes the less organized fighting, the serendipity, and the more unsavory aspects of the Revolution. These authors also tended to accentuate the cynical explanations for why people took up arms and what motivated them to continue. Fortunately, historians have compiled a number of oral histories of the Revolution, interviewing veterans of all sides, and at least one project has been undertaken to reconstruct what it was like in the small communities around the country (Document 22). But everyday life is often left out of the narratives.

The evidence we have indicates that soldiers lived miserable lives. Because resources were scarce, governments were transient and underfunded, and military tactics were a hybrid of guerrilla and standard warfare, the various armies were ragtag. Even worse, many of the soldiers were abducted from their villages or local jails and forced into service. Edith O'Shaughnessy, the wife of a U.S. diplomat, described the reluctant soldiers: "I was startled as I watched the faces of some conscripts marching to the station today. On so many was impressed something desperate and despairing. . . . They often have to be tied to the transport wagons."[3]

Rarely did they wear uniforms. Even the generals did not look like generals. One American observed Villa and Zapata after their victorious entry into Mexico City in 1914: "General Villa [was] wearing an English helmet, a heavy brown sweater, khaki trousers, leggings and heavy riding shoes. Zapata . . . with his immense sombrero . . . wore a short black coat, a large light blue silk neckerchief, [a] pronounced lavender shirt, and used alternatively a white handkerchief with green border and another with all the colors of the flowers. He had on a pair of black tight-fitting Mexican trousers with silver buttons down the outside seam of each leg."[4] Villa's troops were in uniforms bought across the border, while the Zapatistas wore traditional peasant garb, including cotton shirts and huaraches (sandals).

Arms and ammunition consisted of whatever they could obtain. Supply lines were virtually nonexistent, and foraging was the only means of acquiring provisions and shelter. Soldiers often went hungry. Medical care was disastrous. Soldiers badly wounded in battle were almost certain to die. Mostly, the soldiers went unpaid, with the exception of Villa's troops, known as Villistas, from 1913 to 1915. He paid a generous daily wage because his treasury swelled with the proceeds from stolen cattle and mining taxes. He was even able to send wounded veterans back to the state of Chihuahua, where they received pensions, free food, and low-cost beef.

Women known as *soldaderas* made up the supply and medical corps of all the armies. As journalist Elena Poniatowska has observed, "Without the soldaderas there is no Mexican Revolution—they kept it alive and fertile, like the earth."[5] Not only did they feed, clothe, nurse, and bury their men, but they fought bravely alongside them, led them, and died with them. Zapata's army had a unit of female raiders. Women and their children defended Parral, Chihuahua, against the invading U.S. army led by John J. Pershing in 1916, causing the Americans to retreat. There were legendary exploits glorified in the *corridos* (popular songs) of the Revolution (Document 20). And yet, as Poniatowska has also written, "soldaderas ended up with the worst of the Revolution."[6] They did not always join the combat voluntarily. With their men off at war, they had no way to earn a living, and other soldiers sometimes took them from their homes by force. The *soldaderas* rode the military railroads, living in boxcars meant for horses. On the march, they trailed the horses, running to catch up. Generals openly disdained their presence among the troops. Pancho Villa, for example, insisted that they slowed down his cavalry. They were the last priority, rarely protected and usually left to fend for themselves. Moreover, they had no official status. After the Revolution, they received no public recognition, rarely received veterans' pensions, and were largely ignored by historians.

One aspect of the war that profoundly affected the soldiers was the adoption of new military tactics from Europe. The turning point of the civil war between revolutionary factions occurred in 1915 when Obregón began using these tactics. The new warfare consisted of massive numbers of infantry ensconced in trenches with barbed-wire perimeters and machine-gun firepower. Both sides would charge into the enemy's impenetrable defenses, with the result being unprecedented carnage. In the decisive battles of 1915, Villa failed to adopt these tactics, continuing to rely instead on cavalry charges. He suffered horrendous defeats in two battles at Celaya and one at León, including three thousand killed and six thousand taken prisoner at the second Celaya and three thousand more killed at León. The three engagements destroyed Villa's army.

Soldiers also were affected by Carranza's decree of May 14, 1913, in which he proclaimed that anyone "guilty of rebellion against constituted authority, rebellion against established political institutions, or attack on the life of the president" would be subjected to the death penalty.[7] This was the legal basis for the summary execution of prisoners of war, because all federal soldiers were, in Carranza's view, rebelling against established institutions. One likely consequence of this decree was that the fighting would be even more bitter and desperate.

The continous warfare between 1910 and 1920 affected civilians in roughly three stages. The first, from November 1910 to March 1913, involved minimal damages and disruptions except in Chihuahua, Morelos, and a few other scattered places. The heaviest fighting took place in the north, and there was only one major battle, at Ciudad Juárez, near the U.S. border. Casualties in these years were relatively low. Civilians experienced dislocations primarily in northwestern Chihuahua and Ciudad Juárez. Some mining camps suffered raids, and haciendas lost livestock, but most of the elites from the Díaz era remained in Mexico. Luis Terrazas, the country's biggest land and livestock owner and the target of much revolutionary venom, did not go into exile until 1912. The Mormons, who had immigrated from the United States beginning in the 1880s, evacuated the country the same year. In general, however, the economy and everyday life continued as they had before.

This all changed in the second stage, from 1913 to 1917. The country became militarized, as each faction's army expanded in size and absorbed all available provisions and resources, including the railroad system. There was heavy fighting and enormous destruction. Many foreigners returned to their countries of origin. Many industries, notably mining, either ceased operations or continued at a low level of activity. Mining camps were abandoned. Cities such as Mexico City and Veracruz experienced nasty fighting and high casualties.

In the third stage, from 1917 to 1920, the Villistas and Zapatistas reverted to guerrilla warfare. Although they remained dangerous foes of Carranza, he had sufficient control to begin to rebuild. New bandit groups that rose from the large numbers of former soldiers also caused havoc.

Civilians suffered in various ways. Inflation, especially in the price of food, ran rampant. The value of the peso plunged as the competing Villistas and Constitutionalists adopted their own currencies, which they forced everyone in the areas they controlled to use. At one point in 1916, there were twenty-one different "official" paper currencies in circulation.[8] Commonly, merchants refused to accept paper money. Coins, which had intrinsic value because they were made of gold or silver, were scarce for daily transactions. Speculation was wild, and counterfeiters were everywhere, adding to the uncertainty of the value of any currency at any given time.

No matter who held the upper hand militarily, the worst problem every faction faced was the shortage of food. It was almost impossible to ensure an adequate food supply at a reasonable cost. Warfare was hard on agriculture. Armies destroyed or stole crops, equipment, livestock, and seed. Food production declined, exacerbated by the lack of workers, transportation, and irrigation systems, and by equipment in disrepair because of inattention.[9] By mid-1914 in Yucatán, staples were scarce. A plague of locusts brought on near famine.[10] In Veracruz, the price of corn doubled between March and September 1915. In 1914 and 1915, bad luck also intervened in the form of drought in Puebla. In the worst of the fighting between 1914 and 1916, starvation in Mexico City caused its residents to resort to eating cats (Document 22).

As the food crisis intensified, governments tried to redistribute foodstuffs and regulate against hoarding and price gouging. The military impeded such actions by insisting that soldiers receive food before civilians. Unsurprisingly, the generals were entrepreneurs first, above loyalty and duty to their troops, often confiscating and selling staples off for their own profit.[11]

Villages had to adapt quickly to the shifting tides of battle. Rival armies moved back and forth over various territories. One army would arrive, take whatever it could, and depart, succeeded by the opposing army, also in search of supplies. Local police and other officials offered no protection, for they were either off at war or in hiding. On occasion, villagers fought back. One incident in 1915 involving the village of San Pedro de las Cuevas in Chihuahua illustrates just how difficult conditions were in the countryside. The residents there killed Villista troops while defending their homes. In retaliation, Villa massacred sixty villagers, including the local priest, whom he shot himself.[12]

As early as 1912, conditions in Morelos, the scene of some of the heaviest fighting, were horrific. One balladeer described how Huerta's army left the state in ruins:

Our pueblos only plains
White ashes, pictures of horror
Sad deserts, isolated places
Where only sorrow stirs;
Ill-fated remains we venerate
Like relics of our love,
Where we were born, where we were raised
And happily we saw the sunlight.[13]

By 1917, Morelos was a catastrophe: "The hacienda had disappeared, the resident laborers long fled, deported, conscripted or recruited, its fields in corn or weeds, its buildings broken down and burned . . . visible . . . only as a ruin." The villages were no better: "The fields lay empty of crops. . . . In the pastures there were no cattle. Nor were there pigs or chickens. . . . And old local leaders were gone, killed or deported or hiding out. In the misery and disarray bandits reappeared as they always had in such times in Morelos."[14] Conditions there only got worse. In 1918, amid the worldwide influenza outbreak, Morelos lost a quarter of its inhabitants to death and migration.[15]

The cities did not escape calamity. A British diplomat reported how retreating federals in 1916 committed an unspeakable atrocity on Zacatecas, blowing up the city as they fled. "The whole block of buildings . . . is one heap of ruins. [Other buildings] on the opposite side of the street . . . [are] so badly damaged that . . . [they] will have to be taken down. There are hundreds of bodies buried in the debris as at the time of the explosion a great number of federal soldiers was still in the Jefetura. . . . The whole family of Magallanes (twelve or thirteen in number) were blown to pieces. . . . On the plaza the dead were lying everywhere, in many places one on top of the other."[16]

The influx of people from the countryside worsened conditions in the cities, which simply could not feed the new arrivals. Sanitation, never very good, was even more problematic under wartime conditions. Two thousand died from typhus in Puebla in the winter of 1915–1916.[17] Many died from gastrointestinal maladies brought on by contaminated food and water. Contagious diseases were rampant. Local governments struggled incessantly to provide the most basic services and amenities. Deprived of funds, schools were open only sporadically. Everything was in short supply, including housing. Rents also soared, perhaps 50 percent between 1910 and 1922. As a consequence of the alternating invasions of different factions, the movement of people from the countryside, and the influx of single women, prostitution, practiced by otherwise unemployed women, expanded greatly.

For businesspeople in both the countryside and the city, there were effectively no rules. Government policies constantly changed depending on who was in charge. Some army commanders promulgated radical laws that frightened businesspeople. If one had any capital, it was not the time to invest.

The high rate of inflation created a constant demand for higher wages. Clearly, the working class was being squeezed. Workers organized and went on strike. They protested perceived injustices, such as arbitrary deductions from their pay, fines for violations of employers' rules (tardiness, for example), and wage differentials between foreign and Mexican workers. Although there had been union demonstrations and strikes before 1911, the number and extent of these activities rose markedly. Mexico City, of course, was the hotbed of the unions. But other cities, such as Puebla and Orizaba, also led the way. After Díaz fled into exile, the floodgates opened. Nine thousand textile workers struck in January 1912, for example. Within a month, forty thousand were on strike. Pay increases and shorter hours resulted. At the heart of the labor unrest were women. They were particularly active during the Madero years but continued on afterward. Women in the textile, knitwear, and cigarette industries were at the forefront of the labor movement. They helped organize the Casa del Obrero Mundial (House of the Worker of the World), the main labor union organization in the capital.

Women also pushed for their political and social rights. Feminists made their voices heard, organizing the first feminist congress in Yucatán in 1916 (Document 30). One result of their efforts was the Carranza government's decree legalizing divorce in 1914.

Social tensions, including labor unrest, tested the multiclass alliance that made up the Constitutionalists. Coupled with the conflicts over land reform in the countryside, these tensions made it clear that the major issues of the Revolution were far from settled.

THE RESULTS OF THE REVOLUTION

The Revolution profoundly changed Mexico. One could argue that it had accomplished (or would soon accomplish) many, if not all, of its aims. In 1910, the multiclass coalition had set out to achieve two major goals — to reclaim the land taken from the villages by expanding haciendas and greedy politicians, and to open access to government and politics. The latter goal included regaining the local autonomy lost to the central state during the Díaz era. In addition, there were demands for an end to peonage (long-term indebtedness, which bound agricultural laborers to the landowners for whom they worked) and the implementation of higher wages and better working conditions. By 1920, some of these goals had been reached, and the structure was in place to accomplish the rest.

Land reform succeeded in a number of instances, at least for a time, during the decade between 1910 and 1920. The most widely known example occurred in Morelos in 1914, under Zapatista rule. On an informal basis, land reform was already in the works in Zapatista-controlled areas such as the Federal District and the states of Morelos, Puebla, México, and Guerrero. In February 1914, Zapata ordered that the land of enemies of the revolution be divided. Zapata's military returned the land to those who had previously held title to it and redistributed the rest by lottery. All of this land was mapped, and the results were sent to Zapata for his approval.[18] Zapata encountered some resistance to the reform from his local chiefs, who were benefitting from protection money paid by the haciendas. A decree from Zapata in September clarified and codified the reform, but conflicts soon arose because the information available to settle village claims (old manuscripts, maps, and stories) was not sufficient to do so. It was not uncommon for neighboring villages to have rival claims. These disputes often led to violence, so Zapata set up agrarian commissions to settle the claims. The peasant leader was, in effect, adopting methods that Madero might have used — methods that Zapata had rejected only three years earlier.[19] Nonetheless, 1914 and 1915 were the zenith of reform. Despite the many obstacles, villagers had defeated the great landowners and won back their land.

Chihuahua, the birthplace of the Revolution, also experienced radical transformations in landholding at mid-decade. Pancho Villa, at the height of his power and military success, controlled the state in 1914 and 1915. In contrast to his on-again, off-again allies the Zapatistas, Villa grappled with a wider array of problems arising from his decision to battle Carranza and Obregón on the national level. Like Zapata, Villa confronted tremendous pressures to implement land reform. The residents of the old presidios (military colonies) had won the Revolution for Madero and sought the return of their land. Other Chihuahuans demanded the return of property stolen during the land booms of the 1880s and early 1900s, as well as the dismantling of the haciendas and the redistribution of their land. Villa had already expropriated the land of the old oligarchy while fighting for Carranza in 1913. Most notably, he had confiscated the property of the Terrazas family. Villa's dilemma, then, was what to do with the land.

Because the colorful general required enormous resources and manpower to conduct his wars against Huerta and Carranza, the most radical land reform had to wait.[20] With so many Chihuahuan soldiers away from home, the Villista leadership worried that any implementation of reform would leave out the soldiers. Villa also feared that if these same soldiers received land, they would leave the army to go home to work it. In addition, because Villa needed the revenues from the haciendas in Chihuahua (cattle) and Durango (cotton), they would have to continue to operate unimpeded.

His solution was multifaceted. Some of the haciendas were placed under the control of the Administration of Intervened (confiscated) Property of Chihuahua. Others were operated by the state government or local or regional boards. A number of haciendas fell under the control of generals. In most cases, these public entities and officials rented out the haciendas, which was not always beneficial to the resident workers but maintained the needed income. Prior to 1914, there was little improvement in the conditions for laborers on the haciendas, although the Villista administrators took some measures to better their lot. The Villistas also used at least some of the income from the haciendas for social services, especially for the families of soldiers killed in battle.

As for the second goal of the Revolution, opening access to government and politics, the revolutionaries also met with some success. They were able to overturn the closed system of politics and replace the old guard with a new generation of elites, whose membership shifted during the next few decades but who, unlike their Díaz-era predecessors, reached out for mass support (albeit with limitations).[21] Many of the methods of nineteenth-century politics remained, such as cronyism and graft, but access to various opportunities was open to more people.

Local autonomy in the countryside was not easily obtainable. The Zapatistas held elections when they took over a village, but it is not clear just how much leeway local officials had. One civilian politician complained that the revolutionary chiefs had "the erroneous belief that officials must be under the foot of any revolutionary that has no more authority than the power of his arms."[22] Even at the height of Zapata's power in the glorious days of 1914 and 1915, there was the problem of finding "a balance between discipline and village democracy."[23] Although Chihuahuans demanded the restoration of local autonomy, many of them were serving in the army a long way from home. Villa could not hold elections without disenfranchising these soldiers, for they could neither run for office nor vote. As a result, democracy was among the first casualties of war.

The Revolution created space for social activism. Workers in the factories of Mexico City, Puebla, Orizaba, and Guadalajara had their heyday from 1911 through 1917. As we have seen, there was a flurry of strikes during Madero's time, such as on the Mexico City tramways and in the textile factories of Mexico City and Puebla. La Casa del Obrero Mundial was a critical labor union organization during those heady years, actively educating workers and fighting for their rights. It extended its influence when it allied with Carranza and supplied him with the Red Battalions, which helped Obregón defeat Villa in 1915 (Document 27). Symbolic of the organization's brief ascendancy was the fact that its headquarters was in the former home of the elite Jockey Club in downtown Mexico City.[24]

In the immediate sense, as the fighting lessened through 1917 and many soldiers returned home, they found few rewards for their service and sacrifice. Villistas went back to Chihuahua under an amnesty from Carranza, but the land Villa had promised was not forthcoming. Work all over the country was scarce. In Chihuahua, the haciendas had lost most of their cattle, and the mines were still not operating. Carranza's supporters fired Villistas from the state government bureaucracy and were unlikely to hire them in the future.[25] In Morelos, the sugar industry that had employed so many was in ruins. The victory of the Revolution seemed hollow when there were no opportunities to earn a living. It was a bleak outlook indeed.

The Constitution of 1917 was, of course, the most important product of the Revolution between 1910 and 1920. It would form the basis for the next two decades of unprecedented, though erratic and sometimes ineffective, reforms. Despite the varied record of its implementation, to many "the Constitution of 1917 is the legal triumph of the Mexican

Revolution. . . . To some it is the revolution." To these observers, the constitution, underlain by a "humanitarian spirit" and a belief in the "dignity of man,"[26] was the solution to the nation's most critical problems. Three provisions in particular paved the way for extraordinary transformations of Mexican society. Article 3 instilled the national government with the obligation to educate all of its children without cost to them. It also removed the Catholic Church from its formerly dominant role in education. Article 27 claimed land and water as the property of the nation, and as such the nation could distribute them for the public good (Document 31). Article 123 provided workers with a minimum wage, an eight-hour workday, workers' compensation, social security, and the right to organize and strike (Document 32).

The most important provision was Article 27, which established the rights of private property but also gave the government the right to expropriate property for the public good. This article was the expression of a new theory of property, one in which land was correctly in individuals' hands but its private use was always subordinate to the public interest. It gave the state the means to ensure a more equitable distribution of wealth.[27]

The new constitution also provided for unprecedented comprehensive labor legislation. In addition to the rights outlined above, Article 123 mandated overtime pay, a six-day workweek, an end to the payment of wages in scrip, an end to debt peonage, maternity leave, and equal pay regardless of gender. The constitution ended three-quarters of a century of debate about the role of the Roman Catholic Church. It not only removed the church from its role in education, but it also declared the separation of church and state (Article 130) and reduced the church's power by taking away its property. Other constitutional articles limited the number of priests in any state and forbade foreign-born priests.

In sum, the impact of the Revolution was varied. "Informal social change, unplanned and unlegislated, was more significant than formal change."[28] Indeed, the formal changes seemed precarious. The new elections were as corrupt as those in the past. Politics was often violent, with contesting factions frequently employing force of arms to obtain control of local and state governments. Murder was a common tactic for eliminating the opposition. The revolutionaries wrote a constitution that instituted radical changes in the position of the Catholic Church, the role of government in education, the rights of private property owners, and the conditions for working people. But the central authorities more often than not had neither the will nor the power to carry out the constitution's provisions.

For those who benefitted, reform usually carried the price of political obedience. To be sure, the old elites, particularly the landowners, had suffered grievously and would, in the majority, never recover their former status. The new elites, consisting in part of revolutionary military officers, were as corrupt as the old guard. The effect of the upheaval varied widely from region to region and state to state. Conditions also differed radically within each state and within the various parts of each state. While some areas became "laboratories of the Revolution," where revolutionaries passed new laws and regulations improving the lives and working conditions of men, women, and children, others remained virtually untouched.[29] At least temporarily, the Revolution fragmented the nation into the many Mexicos that it had been before the rise of Porfirio Díaz.

INTERNATIONAL RAMIFICATIONS

The Mexican Revolution had far-reaching international implications. During the first decade of the twentieth century, the Great Powers of Europe and the United States competed fiercely for profits and influence in Mexico. The rivalries continued during the Revolution, complicated, of course, by the First World War. The United States was deeply involved in the Revolution not only because Mexico was its neighbor and it was concerned about its own security, but also because U.S. investors had sunk more than a billion dollars into Mexico's railroads, agriculture, mines, and industries. Europeans were heavily invested in Mexico as well, with the British and Germans leading the way in railroads, petroleum, mining, commerce, and ownership of the Mexican government's public debt. French citizens living in Mexico were important industrialists there.

When World War I broke out in 1914, in the midst of the heaviest fighting of the Revolution, the stakes in Mexico grew higher. The United States sought to protect its southern border. Both the United States and Britain took measures to safeguard crucial natural resources supplied by Mexico, especially petroleum. Germany looked to further destabilize Mexico in order to distract the United States from the European war.

Throughout the decade, the United States manipulated the availability of funds, arms, and munitions to Mexico by varying the application of its trade regulations, shutting off supplies to factions of whom it disapproved, or opening up exports to its favorites. The vast U.S. economic interests also worked to protect their holdings. Standard Oil was said to back Madero. The American Smelting and Refining Company, the largest mining operation in Mexico, later cooperated with Villa when he controlled much of the territory in which the firm did business.

In addition, the United States meddled blatantly in Mexican domestic politics and even intervened militarily. The first overt U.S. interference occurred when the U.S. minister to Mexico, Henry Lane Wilson, vigorously opposed Madero because he thought the new president too weak to govern. Wilson went so far as to send misleading, adverse reports about Madero to Washington and to plot against him with General Reyes and Félix Díaz (Document 34).

President Woodrow Wilson interfered openly and sent troops into Mexico on two occasions. First, in 1914, he withheld diplomatic recognition of the Huerta government and shut off its access to arms because it had taken power by undemocratic means. He then sent U.S. warships to the Gulf of Mexico. In April, the U.S. military occupied Mexico's two major Gulf ports, Tampico and Veracruz. Wilson used a minor incident in Tampico, which involved the alleged mistreatment of a U.S. sailor by Mexican authorities, as the reason for the occupation. U.S. troops stayed in Mexico until the end of November, depriving Huerta of the income from customs receipts and access to imported arms and supplies. This put Huerta at a severe disadvantage against the Constitutionalists, who had an open border in the north through which to obtain supplies.

After the defeat of Huerta and the split between Villa and Carranza, the United States was indecisive about whom to support. Villa had treated foreign companies quite well, exacting only occasional, modest taxes. Carranza had demanded much more. When all was said and done, however, the United States sided with the faction that won on the battlefield. Obregón's convincing victories in 1915 led President Wilson to recognize Carranza as the legitimate leader. Villa, in a desperate effort to provoke the United States to invade Mexico and eventually go to war with Carranza (thus shifting the balance of power in Mexico), raided the small town of Columbus, New Mexico, in March 1916, killing two dozen U.S. soldiers and civilians. President Wilson retaliated by sending a large force, led by General John J. Pershing, across the border to hunt down Villa. There were a number of military clashes between U.S. troops and Constitutionalists, one of which led the countries to the brink of war, but Pershing never came close to capturing or defeating Villa. The Americans finally left Mexico in February 1917.

After the withdrawal of these troops, the United States continued to try to influence the course of the Revolution. Obregón overthrew Carranza by force in 1920 (Obregón's soldiers killed Carranza in the process) and subsequently won election as president. The United States withheld diplomatic recognition from the new Obregón government. It was concerned about the regime's attitude toward private property and its treatment of foreign investors, most importantly mining and petroleum companies. These issues were not resolved until 1923, with a compromise, albeit temporary, laid out in the Bucareli Agreements (Document 39). Mexico agreed not to apply Article 27 of the Constitution of 1917—which assigned subsoil rights to the nation—retroactively to properties in operation. The constant tension over who had the rights to Mexican petroleum remained until 1938, when the Mexican government, under President Lázaro Cárdenas, expropriated all foreign oil companies and established Petróleos Mexicanos (PEMEX), a government-owned monopoly.

Perhaps the most important foreign involvement in the Mexican Revolution in terms of its worldwide repercussions was the Zimmermann telegram (Document 36). At the beginning of 1917, after more than two years of stalemate in the European war, German leaders determined that they could gain victory only through unlimited submarine (U-boat) warfare, but they worried that this strategy would likely cause the United States to enter the war against them. Some officials in the German Foreign Office advocated inducing Mexico to attack the United States. They hoped that the United States would then become bogged down in a prolonged guerrilla war. At the time, Pershing's troops were still in Mexico. There had also been some discussion of Germany establishing U-boat bases in Mexico. The Germans thus proposed an alliance in which Mexico could be able to "reconquer" its "lost territory in Texas, New Mexico, and Arizona."

The German foreign minister, Arthur Zimmermann, sent the offer by coded telegram in January 1917. Unfortunately for the Germans, the British had broken the German codes. The British quickly saw that revealing the substance of the telegram to the Americans would help influence them to join the war. On February 24, 1917, the British handed the telegram to the Americans. Carranza ignored the German proposal (in effect rejecting it), never replying or even acknowledging its receipt. Undoubtedly, however, Germany's offer to Mexico contributed to the United States abandoning its policy of neutrality and joining with the Allies.

The Great Powers continued their involvement in Mexico through the end of the Revolution. German corporations purchased mineral

properties and German intelligence gathered information for the war.
The British looked after their petroleum holdings. The French worried
about the enormous public debts from the Díaz regime still owed them.

RECONSTRUCTION

The most violent stage of the Revolution (the subject of this book) came
to a close in 1920. Two more stages remained: first, a period of economic and infrastructure (roads, buildings, communications, water and
sewer systems) reconstruction between 1920 and 1934, incorporating
the presidencies of Alvaro Obregón, Plutarco Elías Calles, and the three
short-term presidents who took office in the wake of the assassination
of Obregón in 1928, just before he was to take office for a second time;
second, the presidency of Lázaro Cárdenas (1934–1940), when the government redistributed tens of millions of acres of land to more than a
million rural dwellers and expropriated the foreign-owned petroleum
companies (1938). Although the decade of violence between 1910 and
1920 had ended the domination of the small ruling class, especially
the large landowners, and severely limited the influence of the Catholic Church, most of the promises of the Revolution—the Constitution
of 1917 notwithstanding—were as yet unfulfilled. Mexico was still a
nation divided along class, gender, racial, and geographic lines. During
the 1920s, revolutionaries slowly pieced together a new mosaic of alliances with regional bosses, the military, organizations of land seekers
and small landowners, and labor unions. In 1929, they formed these alliances into the official political party, the National Revolutionary party.
The regime confronted and defeated three serious rebellions during
this decade. In response to the challenges presented by the revolts, it
carried out some land reform and strengthened labor organizations in
return for the political and military loyalty of rural dwellers and workers. The promise of the Revolution came to fulfillment only with President Cárdenas, who pushed through a vast redistribution of land and
empowered labor unions that won improvements in pay and working
conditions. The sacrifices ordinary Mexicans had made during the violent years of the Revolution were finally redeemed. Some important
reforms, however, such as the right to vote for women (1952), would
have to wait.

The question of whether the Revolution succeeded or failed is a difficult one. Surely millions of Mexicans benefitted from land redistribution and laws bettering their living standards. Others found enormous
opportunities to acquire their fortunes. But the Revolution had caused

widespread death and destruction, and set back economic development decades. If we assess the results of the Revolution in 1940, though, all in all the balance was favorable. During the 1940s a new generation of postrevolutionary leaders, less concerned with social justice and more focused on economic development, took over. The evaluation of the consequences in 2000, when many of the gains of the previous six decades had dissipated over time, was perhaps not as positive. There is no doubt that the Mexican Revolution had forever changed the way Mexicans thought about themselves and their nation.

NOTES

[1] The end date for the Mexican Revolution is a matter of considerable controversy. Some consider that it ended in 1920. Others include the presidencies of Obregón and Calles, identifying the organization of the National Revolutionary party in 1929 as its completion. Still others believe that the Revolution should incorporate the radical reforms of President Cárdenas. Finally, some insist that the Revolution ended in 1946 with the election of President Miguel Alemán Valdés and the rise of a new generation of political leaders.

[2] There were many mixed progeny of the various races. In addition to the blending that produced mestizos and mulattoes, there were mixtures of Indians and Africans and mixtures of all of the various combined descendants.

[3] Edith O'Shaughnessy, *A Diplomat's Wife in Mexico*, quoted in Michael M. Meyer, William L. Sherman, and Susan M. Deeds, *The Course of Mexican History* (New York: Oxford University Press, 2003), 537.

[4] Friedrich Katz, *The Life and Times of Pancho Villa* (Stanford, Calif.: Stanford University Press, 1998), 435.

[5] Elena Poniatowska, *Las Soldaderas: Women of the Mexican Revolution*, trans. David Dorado Romo (El Paso, Tex.: Cinco Punto Press, 2006), 16.

[6] Ibid., 13.

[7] Charles C. Cumberland, *Mexican Revolution: The Constitutionalist Years* (Austin: University of Texas Press, 1972), 74.

[8] David G. LaFrance, *Revolution in Mexico's Heartland: Politics, War, and State Building in Puebla, 1913–1920* (Wilmington, Del.: Scholarly Resources, 2003), 117.

[9] Ibid., 127.

[10] Allen Wells and Gilbert M. Joseph, *Summer of Discontent, Seasons of Upheaval* (Durham, N.C.: Duke University Press, 1996), 264.

[11] LaFrance, *Revolution in Mexico's Heartland*, 130.

[12] Katz, *The Life and Times of Pancho Villa*, 510–11.

[13] Samuel Brunk, *Emiliano Zapata: Revolution and Betrayal in Mexico* (Albuquerque: University of New Mexico Press, 1995), 148.

[14] John Womack Jr., *Zapata and the Mexican Revolution* (New York: Knopf, 1969), 274.

[15] Ibid., 310.

[16] Katz, *The Life and Times of Pancho Villa*, 352.

[17] LaFrance, *Revolution in Mexico's Heartland*, 131.

[18] Brunk, *Emiliano Zapata*, 148, 149.

[19] Ibid., 152–53.

[20] Katz, *The Life and Times of Pancho Villa*, 396–419.

[21] Alan Knight, *The Mexican Revolution* (Cambridge: Cambridge University Press, 1986), 2:514.

[22] Brunk, *Emiliano Zapata*, 155.

[23] Ibid., 169.

[24]John Lear, *Workers, Neighbors, and Citizens: The Revolution in Mexico City* (Lincoln: University of Nebraska Press, 2001), 233.

[25]Katz, *The Life and Times of Pancho Villa*, 551.

[26]E. V. Niemeyer, *Revolution at Querétaro: The Mexican Constitutional Convention of 1916–1917* (Austin: University of Texas Press, 1974), 233–34.

[27]Ibid., 232.

[28]Knight, *The Mexican Revolution*, 2:516.

[29]Thomas Benjamin, "Laboratories of the New State, 1920–1929: Regional Social Reform and Experiments in Mass Politics," in *Provinces of the Revolution: Essays on Regional Mexican History, 1910–1929*, ed. Thomas Benjamin and Mark Wasserman (Albuquerque: University of New Mexico Press, 1990), 71–90.

PART TWO

The Documents

1

The Causes of the Revolution

From its outset in 1910, the Mexican Revolution was extraordinary in that the rebels were made up of a multiclass alliance of middle-sector small merchants; small-business owners; government employees, such as teachers and bureaucrats; peasants, who were small landholders, sharecroppers, tenants, and landless agricultural workers; proletariats, who were urban factory workers and miners; and dissident large landowners. They sought access to politics and fair treatment from the government, return of land expropriated from them as individuals or as villagers, and local autonomy for their villages. Each group sought a different outcome in terms of its own specific interests, but they were united at the start by their desire to oust dictator Porfirio Díaz from office. After the alliance accomplished its initial goals, it disintegrated into warring factions.

1

PARTIDO LIBERAL MEXICANO

The Program of the Mexican Liberal Party

1906

The Partido Liberal Mexicano (Mexican Liberal party), known as the PLM, was the most important precursor of the Mexican Revolution. It was the forerunner of the Revolution in the sense that it won considerable working- and middle-class support in the northern state of Chihuahua. Under the leadership of the Flores Magón brothers, Ricardo and Enrique,

From "Program of the Liberal Party (1906)," in *History of Latin America*, ed. Lewis Hanke (Boston: Little, Brown, 1973), 315–17.

31

the PLM advocated prohibiting presidential reelection, limiting the influence of foreigners, improving wages, and breaking up large landed estates, thus appealing across class lines. The PLM published its own newspaper, Regeneración, *and rebelled briefly and unsuccessfully in 1906.*

The Liberal Party is struggling against the despotism that today rules our country. . . .

Since all the amendments that have been made to the constitution of 1857 by the Government of Porfirio Díaz are considered illegal, it may seem unnecessary to call for the reduction of the presidential term to four years and a ban on re-election. However, these points are so important and were proposed with such unanimity and forcefulness that it has been deemed fitting to include them explicitly in the Program. . . .

Compulsory military service is one of the most odious of tyrannies, incompatible with the rights of the citizen of a free country. This tyranny will be suppressed. . . .

The education of children ought to receive very special attention from a Government which truly desires the advancement of the country. . . . The need to create as many new schools as are required by the country's school-age population will be immediately acknowledged by everyone who is not an enemy of progress. . . .

It is pointless to declare in the Program that the Mexican should be given preference over the foreigner, other conditions being equal, for this is already part of our constitution. As a means of effectively avoiding foreign domination and guaranteeing our territorial integrity, no measure seems more fitting than to consider all foreigners who acquire real estate as Mexican citizens. . . .

The Catholic clergy, exceeding the bounds of its religious mission, has always attempted to make itself a political power and has brought great evils upon the country. . . . Honorable governments . . . will not permit religious encroachments on civil power nor patiently tolerate the continuous rebelliousness of clericalism. . . .

A Government that is interested in the effective welfare of the entire people cannot remain indifferent toward the very important question of labor. Thanks to the Dictatorship of Porfirio Díaz, which puts its power at the service of all the exploiters of the people, the Mexican worker has been reduced to the most wretched conditions. . . .

The rural worker is in an even more deplorable situation than the industrial worker, for he is a veritable serf of the modern feudal lords. . . .

A work day of eight hours and a minimum daily wage of one *peso* is the least that can be sought so that the worker will at least be rescued from poverty, so that fatigue will not drain him of all his energy, and so that he may have the time and desire to seek education and diversion after his work. . . .

The improvement of working conditions on the one hand and, on the other, the equitable distribution of land, with facilities for cultivating and developing it without restrictions, would produce inestimable advance for the nation.

2

JAMES CREELMAN

Interview with Porfirio Díaz
1908

In 1908, at the height of his power and reputation, the seventy-eight-year-old Díaz sat for an interview with the American journalist James Creelman. The interview, published in Pearson's Magazine *in February 1908 and excerpted here, shook Mexican politics to the core. Shockingly, Díaz announced that he would step down from the presidency in 1910 at the end of his term, and he encouraged the formation of political parties to contest the forthcoming election. Mexico, he proclaimed, was ready for democracy. Díaz, of course, quickly changed his mind and stood for reelection in 1910. Nonetheless, the interview spurred a somewhat eccentric scion of a wealthy northern family, Francisco I. Madero, to organize an opposition political party, with him as its presidential candidate. The interview also stimulated other groups within the Porfirian elite to begin considering their options without the aging ruler.*

For twenty-seven years he has governed the Mexican Republic with such power that national elections have become mere formalities. He might easily have set a crown upon his head.

Yet to-day, in the supremacy of his career, this astonishing man — foremost figure of the American hemisphere and unreadable mystery to

From James Creelman, "President Díaz, Hero of the Americas," *Pearson's Magazine*, March 1908, 232–37, 240–42, 244–45.

students of human government—announces that he will insist on retiring from the Presidency at the end of his present term, so that he may see his successor peacefully established and that, with his assistance, the people of the Mexican Republic may show the world that they have entered serenely and preparedly upon the last complete phase of their liberties, that the nation is emerging from ignorance and revolutionary passion, and that it can choose and change presidents without weakness or war. . . .

"It is a mistake to suppose that the future of democracy in Mexico has been endangered by the long continuance in office of one President," he said quietly. "I can say sincerely that the office has not corrupted my political ideals and that I believe democracy to be the one true, just principle of government, although in practice it is possible only to highly developed peoples." . . .

"I can lay down the Presidency of Mexico without a pang of regret, but I cannot cease to serve this country while I live," he added. . . .

". . . I have tried to leave the presidency several times, but it has been pressed upon me and I remained in office for the sake of the nation which trusted me. . . .

"We preserved the republican and democratic form of government. We defended the theory and kept it intact. Yet we adopted a patriarchal policy in the actual administration of the nation's affairs, guiding and restraining popular tendencies, with all full faith that an enforced peace would allow education, industry and commerce to develop elements of stability and unity in a naturally intelligent, gentle and affectionate people.

"I have waited patiently for the day when the people of the Mexican Republic would be prepared to choose and change their government at every election without danger of armed revolutions and without injury to the national credit or interference with national progress. I believe that day has come." . . .

"General Díaz," I interrupted, "you have had an unprecedented experience in the history of republics. For thirty years the destinies of this nation have been in your hands, to mold them as you will; but men will die, while nations must continue to live. Do you expect that Mexico can continue to exist in peace as a republic? Are you satisfied that its future is assured under free institutions?" . . .

"The future of Mexico is assured," he said in a clear voice. "The principles of democracy have not been planted very deep in our people, I fear. But the nation has grown and it loves liberty. Our difficulty has been that the people do not concern themselves enough about public matters for a democracy. The individual Mexican as a rule thinks much about his own rights and is always ready to assert them. But he does not think so much about the rights of others. He thinks of his privileges, but not of his duties. Capacity for self-restraint is the basis of democratic government, and self-restraint is possible only to those who recognize the rights of their neighbors. . . .

"Yet I firmly believe that the principles of democracy have grown and will grow in Mexico." . . .

"It is enough for me that I have seen Mexico rise among the peaceful and useful nations. I have no desire to continue in the Presidency."

3

FRANCISCO I. MADERO

The Plan of San Luis Potosí

1910

After Díaz won the 1910 presidential election, he released his political rival Madero from prison. Madero, fearing that the dictator would imprison him again or kill him, fled to the United States. He subsequently concluded that he could not defeat Díaz through peaceful means and determined instead to rebel. The proclamation stating the reasons for his rebellion, called the Plan of San Luis Potosí, was not particularly radical in its goals, but it nonetheless served as a rallying point for the discontented elements in Mexican society. Peasants, workers, the middle class, and dissident elites joined together under Madero and his plan to rise up against Díaz.

First. The elections for President and Vice President of the Republic, magisitrates of the supreme court of justice of the nation, and deputies and senators, held in June and July of the current year, are declared void.

Second. The present Government of Gen. Diaz is not recognized, as well as all the authorities whose power ought to emanate from the

From "The San Luis Potosí Plan," in United States Senate, Committee on Foreign Relations, *Investigation of Mexican Affairs* (Washington, D.C.: Government Printing Office, 1920), 2:2631–33.

popular vote, because, besides not having been elected by the people, they have lost the few titles of legality they might have by committing . . . the most scandalous electoral fraud recorded in the history of Mexico.

Third. In order to avoid, as far as possible, the upheavals inherent in every revolutionary movement, all the laws promulgated by the present administration and their respective regulations, except those that are manifestly repugnant to the principles proclaimed in this plan, are declared to be in force, with the reservation to amend, in due time, by constitutional methods, those that require amendment. . . .

In every case the obligations contracted by the Porfirist administration with foreign governments and corporations prior to the 20th proximo will be respected.

In abuse of the law on public lands numerous proprietors of small holdings, in their greater part Indians, have been dispossessed of their lands by rulings of the department of public development . . . or by decisions of the tribunals of the Republic. As it is just to restore to their former owners the lands of which they were dispossessed in such an arbitrary manner, such rulings and decisions are declared subject to revision, and those who have acquired them in such an immoral manner, or their heirs, will be required to restore them to their former owners, to whom they shall also pay an indemnity for the damages suffered. Solely in case those lands have passed to third persons before the promulgation of this plan shall the former owners receive an indemnity from those in whose favor the dispossession was made.

Fourth. Besides the constitution and existing laws, the principle of no reelection of the President and Vice President of the Republic, governors of the States, and municipal presidents is declared to be the supreme law of the Republic until the respective constitutional amendments are made.

Fifth. I assume the character of provisional President of the United States of Mexico, with the necessary powers to make war on the usurping government of Gen. Diaz.

As soon as the capital of the Republic and more than half of the States of the federation are in the power of the forces of the people the provisional President will issue a call for extraordinary general elections one month thereafter, and shall deliver the power to the President who is elected as soon as the result of the election is known. . . .

Seventh. The 20th day of the month of November, after 6 p.m., all citizens of the Republic will take up arms to remove from power all the authorities who now govern it. (The towns which are at distance from means of communication will do so the day previous.) . . .

Fellow citizens, if I call upon you to take up arms and overthrow the government of Gen. Diaz, it is not only because of the unwarranted act he committed during the last elections, but to save the country from the gloomy future that awaits it under his dictatorship and under the government of the nefarious scientific oligarchy which, without scruple and in great haste, are absorbing and wasting the national resources, and, if we permit him to continue in power, in a very short time they will have completed their work; they will have led the people into ignominy and will have degraded them; they will have sucked all their wealth and left them in the most absolute misery; they will have caused the bankruptcy of our finances and the dishonor of our country which, weak, impoverished, and manacled, will find itself without arms to defend its frontiers, its honor, and its institutions.

In so far as concerns me, I have a tranquil conscience, and no one can accuse me of promoting the revolution for personal ends, for it is within the knowledge of the nation that I did everything possible to reach a peaceable arrangement. . . .

He himself justified the present revolution when he said, "Let no citizen impose and perpetuate himself in the exercise of power, and this will be the last revolution."

FRANCISCO I. MADERO.
San Luis Potosí, *October 5, 1910.*

4

EMILIANO ZAPATA

The Plan of Ayala

1911

The most prominent peasant element of the revolution arose in the state of Morelos, just south of Mexico City. Its head, Emiliano Zapata, had begun as the leader of a small village that sought to recover land expropriated by the neighboring large estate. Zapata and his followers joined with the Madero movement in 1910. But the Morelos peasants did not fully

From Emiliano Zapata et al., "Plan of Ayala," in *Revolution in Mexico: Years of Upheaval, 1910–1940*, ed. James W. Wilkie and Albert L. Michaels (Tucson: University of Arizona Press, 1984), 45–46.

trust Madero. When it appeared that he would not proceed quickly with land redistribution after his victory over Díaz and his election as president, the Zapatistas rebelled against him, issuing the Plan of Ayala only three weeks after he took office. Zapata's protest and revolt were striking evidence that the revolutionary coalition had shattered because of the conflicting goals of various groups in the multiclass alliance. Madero, representing the middle and upper classes, was concerned with political and legal processes and the protection of private property rights, while the Zapatistas sought the prompt redistribution of land.

We, the undersigned, constituted as a Revolutionary Junta, in order to support and fulfill the promises made by the Revolution of November 20, 1910, solemnly proclaim . . . the following plan:

. . . We declare the said Francisco I. Madero unfit to realize the promises of the Revolution of which he is the author, because he is a traitor to the principles . . . which enabled him to climb to power . . . and because, in order to please the *científicos, hacendados,*[1] and *caciques*[2] who enslave us, he has crushed with fire and blood those Mexicans who seek liberties.

*　　*　　*

The Revolutionary Junta of the State of Morelos will not sanction any transactions or compromises until it secures the downfall of the dictatorial elements of Porfirio Díaz and Francisco I. Madero, because the nation is tired of traitors and false liberators who make promises and forget them when they rise to power . . . as tyrants.

As an additional part of the plan that we proclaim, be it known: that the lands, woods, and water usurped by the hacendados, científicos, or caciques, under the cover of tyranny and venal justice, henceforth belong to the towns or citizens in possession of the deeds concerning these properties of which they were despoiled through the devious action of our oppressors. The possession of said properties shall be kept at all costs, arms in hand. The usurpers who think they have a right to said goods may state their claims before special tribunals to be established upon the triumph of the Revolution.

---

[1] *hacendados*: owners of large estates.
[2] *caciques*: Originally, *cacique* was the word for an indigenous local leader, but eventually it came to be used for any local political boss.

... The immense majority of Mexico's villages and citizens own only the ground on which they stand. They suffer the horrors of poverty without being able to better their social status in any respect, or without being able to dedicate themselves to industry or agriculture due to the fact that the lands, woods, and water are monopolized by a few. For this reason, through prior compensation, one-third of such monopolies will be expropriated from their powerful owners in order that the villages and citizens of Mexico may obtain *ejidos*,[3] colonies, town sites, and rural properties for sowing or tilling, and in order that the welfare and prosperity of the Mexican people will be promoted in every way.

The property of those hacendados, científicos, or caciques who directly or indirectly oppose the present plan shall be nationalized, and two-thirds of their remaining property shall be designated for war indemnities—pensions for the widows and orphans of the victims that succumb in the struggle for this plan.

[3] *ejidos*: Landholdings held collectively by a village.

5

FRANCISCO "PANCHO" VILLA

Dreams for a Future Mexico

ca. 1913

Francisco "Pancho" Villa was, perhaps, the most notorious revolutionary leader and most certainly the most controversial. Historians have labeled him as everything from a murderous bandit to a great reformer. Villa represented the middle-class, peasant, and working-class segments of the revolutionary movement. He had been at various times a muleteer (hauling ore and mining supplies), a small-business operator, and an outlaw. Villa was a mercurial figure and a tough, at times brutal, military leader. But he had a vision for the future and a sincere affection for his loyal soldiers. All of this comes through in the unpublished parts of his memoirs. This selection outlines Villa's dream, helping us to understand why he and his followers rebelled and continued to fight.

From Francisco Villa, unpublished memoir, quoted in Friedrich Katz, *The Secret War in Mexico* (Chicago: University of Chicago Press, 1981), 280–81.

And I see that orderly grouping of little houses in which soldiers/farmers live: clean and white, smiling and hygienic, the true homes for which one really fights with courage and for whose defense one would die.

I see these luxurious fruit orchards, these abundant vegetable gardens, these sown fields, these corn fields, these alfalfa fields which not only a *large landowner harvests* and *accrues* benefits from but rather an entire family *cultivates* and *gathers, cares for, and harvests.*

And I see that the school is the tallest building in the hamlet and the teacher is the most respected man; and that the one who studies and knows the most is the most appreciated youth; and that the happiest father is he who will leave his land, animals, and house to his learned, good, and honest child, so that new, healthy, learned, good, hard-working children will arise from this sanctified home, who will dignify the country and honor the race.

Oh, if life will only permit me to live long enough to see this dream realized! . . . The true army of the people, which I loved so much, dispersed through the entire land, plowing the soil, making it respectable and respected! Fifteen years! Twenty years, perhaps! And the sons of my soldiers, who will bring this ideal to fruition will know with what tenderness I caressed this dream of my soul. And they will not suffer, they will not have the threat of suffering, which I endured in the fullest years of my life, which formed my youth and my entire maturity.

6

JOHN KENNETH TURNER

Barbarous Mexico

1910

Although the Mexican Revolution originated in considerable part because of injustices perpetrated by the Díaz regime in the countryside, particularly the expropriations of village land and the national government's incursions against local autonomy, not all peasants rebelled. In fact, the people who were the most badly treated were the least likely to take up

From John Kenneth Turner, *Barbarous Mexico* (Chicago: Charles H. Kerr, 1910), 12–28, 30–32.

*arms. Such was the case in the henequen plantations of Yucatán, where
Yaquis deported from Sonora and Mayas from the local regions were
enslaved. Henequen, the fiber from a species of the agave plant, had
become an important export crop because it yielded twine used for tying
up wheat in harvesting machines. John Kenneth Turner was a muckrak-
ing American journalist who traveled in Mexico during the last years of
the Díaz regime, and who discovered and publicized shocking conditions
on henequen plantations. This excerpt shows just how vicious the treatment of indigenous peoples was under Díaz.*

Slavery in Mexico! Yes, I found it. I found it first in Yucatan. The peninsula of Yucatan is an elbow of Central America, which shoots off in a
northeasterly direction almost half way to Florida. . . .

. . . The surface of the state is almost solid rock, so nearly solid that
it is usually impossible to plant a tree without first blasting a hole to
receive the shoot and make a place for the roots. Yet this naturally barren land is more densely populated than is our own United States. More
than that, within one-fourth of the territory three-fourths of the people
live, and the density of the population runs to nearly seventy-five per
square mile.

The secret of these peculiar conditions is that the soil and the climate
of northern Yucatan happen to be perfectly adapted to the production
of that hardy species of century plant which produces *henequen*, or sisal
hemp. Hence we find the city of Merida, a beautiful modern city claiming a population of 60,000 people, and surrounding it, supporting it, vast
henequen plantations on which the rows of gigantic green plants extend
for miles and miles. The farms are so large that each has a little city of
its own, inhabited by from 500 to 2,500 people, according to the size of
the farm. The owners of these great farms are the chief slave-holders
of Yucatan; the inhabitants of the little cities are the slaves. . . . The slave-
holders' club numbers 250 members, but the vast majority of the lands
and the slaves are concentrated in the hands of fifty henequen kings.
The slaves number more than one hundred thousand. . . .

Chief among the henequen kings of Yucatan is Olegario Molina, former governor of the state and Secretary of Fomento (Public Promo-
tion) of Mexico. Molina's holdings of lands in Yucatan and Quintana Roo
aggregate 15,000,000 acres, or 23,000 square miles—a small kingdom
in itself. The fifty kings live in costly palaces in Merida and many of
them have homes abroad. They travel a great deal, usually they speak

several different languages, and they and their families are a most cultivated class of people. All Merida and all Yucatan, even all the peninsula
of Yucatan, are dependent on the fifty henequen kings. Naturally these
men are in control of the political machinery of their state, and naturally they operate that machinery for their own benefit. The slaves are
8,000 Yaqui Indians imported from Sonora, 3,000 Chinese (Koreans),
and between 100,000 and 125,000 native Mayas, who formerly owned
the lands that the henequen kings now own.

The Maya people, indeed, form about ninety-five per cent of the population of Yucatan. . . .

The planters do not call their chattels slaves. They call them "people,"
or "laborers," especially when speaking to strangers. But when speaking confidentially they have said to me: "Yes, they are slaves."

But I did not accept the word slavery from the people of Yucatan,
though they were the holders of the slaves themselves. The proof of a
fact is to be found, not in the name, but in the conditions thereof. Slavery
is the ownership of the body of a man, an ownership so absolute that
the body can be transferred to another, an ownership that gives to the
owner a right to take the products of that body, to starve it, to chastise it
at will, to kill it with impunity. Such is slavery in the extreme sense. Such
is slavery as I found it in Yucatan.

The masters of Yucatan do not call their system slavery; they call it
enforced service for debt. . . .

But the fact that it is not service for debt is proven by the habit of
transferring the slaves from one master to another, not on any basis of
debt, but on the basis of the market price of a man. In figuring on the
purchase of a plantation I always had to figure on paying cash for the
slaves, exactly the same as for the land, the machinery and the cattle.
Four hundred Mexican dollars apiece was the prevailing price. . . .

The Yaquis are transferred on exactly the same basis as the
Mayas—the market price of a slave—and yet all people of Yucatan
know that the planters pay only $65 apiece to the government for each
Yaqui.[1] . . .

Even then, I thought, it would not be so bad if the servant had an
opportunity of working out the price and buying back his freedom. . . .

But I found that such was not the custom. "You need have no fear
in purchasing this plantation," said one planter to me, "of the laborers being able to buy their freedom and leave you. They can never do
that.". . .

---

[1] The government conducted a war against the Yaqui people for decades. The army
deported captured Yaquis to Yucatán. The generals sold them to plantation owners.

How are the slaves recruited? Don Joaquin Peon informed me that the Maya slaves die off faster than they are born, and Don Enrique Camara Zavala told me that two-thirds of the Yaquis die during the first year of their residence in the country. Hence the problem of recruiting the slaves seemed to me a very serious one. . . .

"It is very easy," one planter told me. "All that is necessary is that you get some free laborer in debt to you, and then you have him. Yes, we are always getting new laborers in that way." . . .

So we see that the debt element in Yucatan not only does not palliate the condition of the slave, but rather makes it harder. It increases his extremity, for while it does not help him to climb out of his pit, it reaches out its tentacles and drags down his brother, too. . . . Let a family, however virtuous, however worthy, however cultivated, fall into misfortune, let the parents fall into debt and be unable to pay the debt, and the whole family is liable to pass into the hands of a henequen planter. Through debt, the dying slaves of the farms are replaced by the unsuccessful wage-workers of the cities.

. . . Service for debt in a milder form than is found in Yucatan exists all over Mexico and is called peonage. Under this system, police authorities everywhere recognize the right of an employer to take the body of a laborer who is in debt to him, and to compel the laborer to work out the debt. Of course, once the employer can compel the laborer to work, he can compel him to work at his own terms, and that means that he can work him on such terms as will never permit the laborer to extricate himself from his debt.

Such is peonage as it exists throughout all Mexico. In the last analysis it is slavery, but the employers control the police, and the fictional distinction is kept up all the same. Slavery is peonage carried to its greatest possible extreme, and the reason we find the extreme in Yucatan is that, while in some other sections of Mexico a fraction of the ruling interests are opposed to peonage and consequently exert a modifying influence upon it, in Yucatan all the ruling interests are in henequen. The cheaper the worker the higher the profits for all. The peon becomes a chattel slave. . . .

The slaves of Yucatan get no money. They are half starved. They are worked almost to death. They are beaten. A large percentage of them are locked up every night in a house resembling a jail. If they are sick they must still work, and if they are so sick that it is impossible for them to work, they are seldom permitted the services of a physician. The women are compelled to marry, compelled to marry men of their own plantation only, and sometimes are compelled to marry certain men not of their choice. There are no schools for the children. Indeed, the entire lives of these people are ordered at the whim of a master, and if the master wishes to kill them, he may do so with impunity. . . .

The philosophy of beating [slaves] was made very clear to me by Don Felipe G. Canton, secretary of the Camara.[2]

"It is necessary to whip them—oh, yes, very necessary," he told me, with a smile, "for there is no other way to make them do what you wish. What other means is there of enforcing the discipline of the farm? If we did not whip them they would do nothing." . . .

One of the first sights we saw on a henequen plantation was the beating of a slave—a formal beating before the assembled toilers of the ranch early in the morning just after the daily roll call. The slave was taken on the back of a huge Chinaman and given fifteen lashes across the bare back with a heavy, wet rope, lashes so lustily delivered that the blood ran down the victim's body. This method of beating is an ancient one in Yucatan and is the customary one on all the plantations for boys and all except the heaviest men. Women are required to kneel to be beaten, as sometimes are men of great weight. Men and women are beaten in the fields as well as at the morning roll call. Each foreman, or *capataz*, carries a heavy cane with which he punches and prods and whacks the slaves at will. I do not remember visiting a single field in which I did not see some of this punching and prodding and whacking going on. . . .

The great plantations of Yucatan are reached by private mule car lines built and operated specially for the business of the henequen kings. The first plantation that we visited was typical. Situated fifteen miles west of Merida, it contains thirty-six square miles of land, one-fourth of it in henequen, part of the rest in pasture and a part unreclaimed. . . .

Here we found fifteen hundred slaves and about thirty bosses of various degrees. Thirty of the slaves were Koreans, about two hundred were Yaquis and the rest were Mayas. The Maya slaves, to my eyes, differed from the free Mayas I had seen in the city principally in their clothing and their general unkempt and overworked appearance. . . . Their clothing was poor and ragged, yet generally clean. The women wore calico, the men the thin, unbleached cotton shirt and trousers of the tropics, the trousers being often rolled to the knees. Their hats were of coarse straw or grass, their feet always bare.

Seven hundred of the slaves are able-bodied men, the rest women and children. Three hundred and eighty of the men are married and live with their families in the one-room huts. These huts are set in little

[2] *Camara*: Camara de Agricola, or planters organization.

patches of ground 144 feet square, which, rocky and barren as they are, are cultivated to some small purpose by the women and children. In addition to the product of their barren garden patch each family receives daily credit at the plantation store for twenty-five *centavos*, or twelve and one-half cents' worth of merchandise. No money is paid; it is all in credit, and this same system prevails on about one-half the plantations. The other half merely deal out rations. It amounts to the same thing, but some of the planters stick to the money credit system merely in order to keep up the pretense of paying wages. I priced some of the goods at the store — corn, beans, salt, peppers, clothing and blankets was about all there was — and found that the prices were high. I could not understand how a family could live on twelve and one-half cents' worth of it each day, a hard-working family, especially.

The slaves rise from their beds when the big bell in the *patio* rings at 3:45 o'clock in the morning, and their work begins as soon thereafter as they can get to it. Their work in the fields ends when it is too dark to see, and about the yards it sometimes extends until long into the night.

The principal labor of the plantation is harvesting the henequen leaves and cleaning the weeds from between the plants. Each slave is given a certain number of leaves to cut or plants to clean, and it is the policy of the planter to make the stint so hard that the slave is compelled to call out his wife and children to help him. Thus nearly all the women and children of the plantation spend a part of the day in the field. The unmarried women spend all the day in the field, and when a boy reaches the age of twelve he is considered to be a man and is given a stint of his own to do. Sundays the slaves do not work for the master. They spend their time in their patches, rest or visit. Sunday is the day on which the youths and maidens meet and plan to marry. Sometimes they are even permitted to go off the farm and meet the slaves of their neighbor, but never are they permitted to marry the people of other plantations, for this would necessitate the purchase of either the wife or the husband by one or the other of the two owners, and that would involve too much trouble.

Such are the conditions in general that prevail on all the plantations of Yucatan.

We spent two days and two nights on the plantation called San Antonio Yaxche and became thoroughly acquainted with its system and its people. . . .

More than three hundred of the able-bodied slaves spend the nights in a large structure of stone and mortar, surrounded by a solid wall twelve feet high, which is topped with the sharp edges of thousands of broken glass bottles. To this inclosure there is but one door, and at it stands a guard armed with a club, a sword and a pistol. . . .

I sampled the supper of the slaves. That is, I sampled a part of it with my tongue, and the rest, which my nostrils warned me not to sample with my tongue, I sampled with my nostrils. The meal consisted of two large corn *tortillas*, the bread of the poor of Mexico, a cup of boiled beans, unflavored, and a bowl of fish—putrid, stinking fish, fish that reeked with an odor that stuck in my system for days. How could they ever eat it? Ah, well, to vary a weary, unending row of meals consisting of only beans and *tortillas* a time must come when the most refined palate will water to the touch of something different, though that something is fish which offends the heavens with its rottenness.

"Beans, *tortillas*, fish! I suppose that they can at least keep alive on it," I told myself, "provided they do no worse at the other two meals." "By the way," I turned to the *administrador*, who was showing us about, "what do they get at the other two meals?"

"The other two meals?" The *administrador* was puzzled. "The other two meals? Why, there aren't any others. This is the only meal they have!"

Beans, *tortillas*, fish, once a day, and a dozen hours under the hottest sun that ever shone!

"But, no," the *administrador* corrected himself. "They do get something else, something very fine, too, something that they can carry to the field with them and eat when they wish. Here is one now."

At this he picked up from one of the tables of the women a something about the size of his two small fists, and handed it to me, triumphantly. I took the round, soggy mass in my fingers, pinched, smelled and tasted it. It proved to be corn dough, half fermented and patted into a ball. This, then, was the other two meals, the rest of the substance besides beans, *tortillas* and decayed fish which sustained the toilers throughout the long day.

7

B. TRAVEN

Corruption

1931

B. Traven's novel Government, *published in 1931, depicts the intense inequities of the Díaz era, exploring the tyranny of local rule and the exploitation of Indians by local officials. The grievances against the Díaz regime and its allies on the state and local levels were due primarily to the loss of local autonomy. Villagers deeply resented that the dictatorship had limited or taken away their long-held rights to use communal land, levy taxes, and govern themselves. These indigenous peoples despised the intrusion of central authority into their everyday lives and traditions. Unlike the enslaved Indians of Yucatán, many villagers in Morelos and other parts of the nation rebelled in 1910 and continued to fight for land and liberty through the following decade.*

Under the regime of the dictatorship the Mexican had nothing else before his eyes from childhood but an officialdom that regarded public office only as a means of enriching itself. The people were taught nothing else and they heard nothing else. If an official was spoken of, it was not "The man has a difficult and responsible post" but "The man has rounded up his sheep, he has only to shear them—he's a governor." And from early youth don Gabriel had learned that even the smallest post had to yield an income far in excess of the salary.

The dictator, don Porfirio [Díaz], had astonished the world by showing in a brief space of time that the bankrupt Republic of Mexico was so flourishing that other countries could only envy its bursting treasury. It was proved by the statistics, which proved also that a great statesman had brought the Mexican people to a level of civilization and prosperity which no one would have thought possible. He knew how to keep national expenditure down to a ridiculously low figure. That was easy. Official salaries were in many cases so small that a mouse could scarcely have lived on them; and if a government inspector or a judge wanted to

From B. Traven, *Government* (Chicago: Ivan R. Dee, 1993), 71–72.

live in a manner befitting his station, he had to find some other source of income as well. It went without saying that he used his power to enlarge this other source to the utmost. The treasury grew richer and richer, the national debt, on paper, smaller and smaller; the poverty of the people, ignorance, corruption, and shameless injustice were, on the other hand, more and more widely diffused.

Don Gabriel knew that he was given his post as a means to enrich himself, and that he was not given it to promote the well-being of an Indian village and its inhabitants. All he lacked was the adroitness and cunning to squeeze out the last drop the job could yield.

He would never have seen that a convoy of Indian laborers passing through the place could put sixteen pesos in his pocket if his brother Mateo had not demonstrated it. Don Mateo had a rich store of experience, gleaned from his life among other officials. It was not experience only, however, that inspired don Mateo, but—what an official needed even more—imagination and resourcefulness.

"If a job brings nothing in," he said to don Gabriel ten times a day, "then you must make it bring something in."

8

JOSÉ GUADALUPE POSADA

The Bloody Events in the City of Puebla

1910

There was considerable political agitation throughout Mexico as a result of Francisco Madero's unsuccessful campaign for the presidency in 1910. Tensions rose in November as Madero made plans to rebel. In Puebla, a state just east of Mexico City, there was a conspiracy to overthrow the Díaz regime that the dictator's police discovered. On November 18, the conspirators were killed, producing the first martyrs of the Revolution. The police chief there, Miguel Cabrera, a notoriously brutal convicted murderer, also was killed in the raid. In this broadsheet, José Guadalupe Posada, a printmaker known for his illustrations in the popular press in

José Guadalupe Posada, "Los sangrientos sucesos en la Ciudad de Puebla," Amon Carter Museum of Modern Art, Fort Worth, Texas.

Mexico City, depicts the death of Cabrera in such a way as to indirectly acknowledge the chief's reputation for oppressing the people of Puebla. The heading reads, "The Bloody Events in the City of Puebla. The death of the Police Chief Miguel Cabrera." It is ironic that Posada chose to portray a well-known villain rather than one of the fallen revolutionaries.

2

At War

The military history of the Revolution can be divided roughly into four phases. The combat began as guerrilla warfare in Chihuahua, the northern state just below El Paso, Texas. The first phase ended with the siege and surrender of Ciudad Juárez in May 1911 and Díaz's exile. There followed a year or so of guerrilla warfare in the south and Pascual Orozco's revolt in the north. During the third phase, 1913 to 1915, conventional warfare with large battles predominated, although the Zapatistas and others carried on a continuous guerrilla struggle in the regions south of Mexico City. The largest, bloodiest battles were fought during these years. Alvaro Obregón's destruction of Pancho Villa's army in 1915 and Zapata's retreat led to the fourth stage, more guerrilla warfare, which lasted until 1920, when Villa at last laid down his arms.

9

JOHN REED

Villa's Rules of War

1914

Pancho Villa seemed indestructible in 1914 as he crushed the federal army, led by General (and President) Victoriano Huerta. Always colorful and sometimes murderous, Villa was a magnet for newspaper correspondents from all over the world, especially the United States. One of the most famous journalists of the early twentieth century, John Reed, got his start reporting on the Mexican Revolution and Villa. Reed's book

From John Reed, *Insurgent Mexico* (New York: Appleton, 1914), 140–44.

Insurgent Mexico *was derived from stories that originally appeared in the* Metropolitan Magazine *in 1913 and 1914. Reed covered Villa's stunning campaign against Huerta, who had overthrown and killed Francisco Madero, the first head of the Revolution, in 1913. Villa was popularly known for his boldness on the battlefield. In this selection, Reed presents him as a tactical innovator who "invented" nighttime attacks and hospital railroad cars and employed quick mobility to overcome his enemies. Reed, like the great novelist Mariano Azuela, gets to the grit and the emotions of an army on the move.*

Villa had to invent an entirely original method of warfare, because he never had a chance to learn anything of accepted military strategy. In that he is without the possibility of any doubt the greatest leader Mexico has ever had. . . . Secrecy, quickness of movement, the adaptation of his plans to the character of the country and of his soldiers,—the value of intimate relations with the rank and file, and of building up a tradition among the enemy that his army is invincible, and that he himself bears a charmed life,—these are his characteristics. He knew nothing of accepted European standards of strategy or of discipline. One of the troubles of the Mexican federal army is that its officers are thoroughly saturated with conventional military theory. The Mexican soldier is . . . , above all, a loose, individual, guerrilla fighter. Red-tape simply paralyzes the machine. When Villa's army goes into battle he is not hampered by salutes, or rigid respect for officers, or trigonometrical calculations of the trajectories of projectiles, or theories of the percentage of hits in a thousand rounds of rifle fire, or the function of cavalry, infantry and artillery in any particular position, or rigid obedience to the secret knowledge of its superiors. . . . But he does know that guerrilla fighters cannot be driven blindly in platoons around the field in perfect step, that men fighting individually and of their own free will are braver than long volleying rows in the trenches, lashed to it by officers with the flat of their swords. And where the fighting is fiercest—when a ragged mob of fierce brown men with hand bombs and rifles rush the bullet-swept streets of an ambushed town—Villa is among them, like any common soldier.

Up to his day, Mexican armies had always carried with them hundreds of the women and children of the soldiers; Villa was the first man to think of swift forced marches of bodies of cavalry, leaving their women behind. Up to his time no Mexican army had ever abandoned its base; it had always stuck closely to the railroad and the supply trains. But Villa struck terror into the enemy by abandoning his trains and throwing his entire effective army upon the field, as he did at Gomez Palacio. He invented in Mexico that most demoralizing form of battle—the night attack. When, after the fall of Torreon last September, he withdrew his entire army in the face of Orozco's advance from Mexico City and for five days unsuccessfully attacked Chihuahua, it was a terrible shock to the Federal General when he waked up one morning and found that Villa had sneaked around the city under cover of darkness, captured a freight train at Terrazzas and descended with his entire army upon the comparatively undefended city of Juarez. It wasn't fair! Villa found that he hadn't enough trains to carry all his soldiers, even when he had ambushed and captured a Federal troop train, sent south by General Castro, the Federal commander in Juarez. So he telegraphed that gentleman as follows, signing the name of the Colonel in command of the troop train: "Engine broken down at Moctezuma. Send another engine and five cars." The unsuspecting Castro immediately dispatched a new train. Villa then telegraphed him: "Wires cut between here and Chihuahua. Large force of rebels approaching from south. What shall I do?" Castro replied: "Return at once." And Villa obeyed, telegraphing cheering messages at every station along the way. The Federal commander got wind of his coming about an hour before he arrived, and left, without informing his garrison, so that, outside of a small massacre, Villa took Juarez almost without a shot. And with the border so near he managed to smuggle across enough ammunition to equip his almost armless forces and a week later sallied out and routed the pursuing Federal forces with great slaughter at Tierra Blanca.

General Hugh L. Scott, in command of the American troops at Fort Bliss, [Texas,] sent Villa a little pamphlet containing the Rules of War adopted by the Hague Conference. He spent hours poring over it. It interested and amused him hugely. He said: ". . . It seems to me a funny thing to make rules about war. It's not a game. What is the difference between civilized war and any other kind of war? . . ."

As far as I could see, the Rules of War didn't make any difference in Villa's original method of fighting. The *colorados*[1] he executed wherever he captured them; because, he said, they were peons like the Revolutionists and that no peon would volunteer against the cause of liberty unless he were bad. The Federal officers also he killed, because, he explained, they were educated men and ought to know better. But the Federal common soldiers he set at liberty because most of them were

---

[1] *colorados*: The followers of Pascual Orozco, who rebelled against Madero in 1912.

conscripts, and thought that they were fighting for the Patria [fatherland]. There is no case on record where he wantonly killed a man. . . .

. . . Villa, although he had never heard of the Rules of War, carried with his army the only field hospital of any effectiveness that any Mexican army has ever carried. It consisted of forty box-cars enameled inside, fitted with operating tables and all the latest appliances of surgery, and manned by more than sixty doctors and nurses. Every day during the battle shuttle trains full of the desperately wounded ran from the front to the base hospitals at Parral, Jimenez and Chihuahua. He took care of the Federal wounded just as carefully as of his own men. Ahead of his own supply train went another train, carrying two thousand sacks of flour, and also coffee, corn, sugar, and cigarettes to feed the entire starving population of the country around Durango City and Torreon.

The common soldiers adore him for his bravery and his coarse, blunt humor. Often I have seen him slouched on his cot in the little red caboose in which he always traveled, cracking jokes familiarly with twenty ragged privates sprawled on the floor, chairs and tables. When the army was entraining or detraining, Villa personally would be on hand in a dirty old suit, without a collar, kicking mules in the stomach and pushing horses in and out of the stock-cars.

10

JOHN REED

The Horrors of Battle

1914

John Reed was not one to observe from a position of safety. He ventured onto the battlefield. In this selection from chapters titled "The Bloody Dawn," and "Battle," he illustrates the horrors of war, from the unending noise of the battlefield to the terror of hand-to-hand combat. The soldiers seem to have been perpetually afraid, hungry, and exhausted. We can also discern a hint of disillusionment among both soldiers and civilians as the war continued longer than anyone had anticipated.

From John Reed, *Insurgent Mexico* (Appleton, 1914), 208–12, 214–15, 220–29.

The Bloody Dawn

The steady noise of battle filled all the night. Ahead torches danced, rails clanged, sledges drummed on the spikes, the men of the repair gang shouted in the frenzy of their toil. It was after twelve. Since the trains had reached the beginning of the torn track we had made half a mile. Now and then a straggler from the main body came down the line of trains, shuffled into the light with his heavy Mauser [rifle] awry across his shoulders, and faded into the darkness toward the debauch of sound in the direction of Gomez Palacio. The soldiers of our guard, squatting about their little fires in the fields, relaxed their tense expectancy. . . .

It was bitter cold. We threw our blankets around us, serape fashion, and trudged down past the fury of the repair gang as they hammered at it under the leaping flares — past the five armed men slouching around their fire on the frontier of the dark.

"Are you off to the battle, *compañeros?*" cried one of the gang. "Look out for the bullets!" At that they all laughed. The sentries cried, "*Adios! Don't kill them all!* . . ."

. . . We stumbled along over the broken track, silently, just able to make him out with our eyes. He was a little dumpy soldier with a rifle and a half-empty cartridge-belt over his breast. He said that he had just brought a wounded man from the front to the hospital train and was on his way back.

"Feel this," he said, holding out his arm. It was drenched. We could see nothing.

"Blood," he continued unemotionally. "His blood. He was my *compadre* in the Brigada Gonzales-Ortega. We went in this night down there and so many, so many — We were cut in half."

It was the first we had heard, or thought, of wounded men. All of a sudden we heard the battle. It had been going on steadily all the time, but we had forgotten — the sound was so monstrous, so monotonous. Far rifle fire came like the ripping of strong canvas, the cannon shocked like pile-drivers. We were only six miles away now.

Out of the darkness loomed a little knot of men — four of them — carrying something heavy and inert in a blanket slung between. Our guide threw up his rifle and challenged, and his answer was a retching groan from the blanket.

"*Oiga compadre,*" lisped one of the bearers huskily, "Where, for the love of the Virgin, is the hospital train?" . . .

Under two tall cotton-wood trees beside an irrigation ditch a little fire glowed. Three sleepers with empty cartridge-belts sprawled snoring on the uneven ground; beside the fire sat a man holding with both hands his leg straight out to the warmth. It was a perfectly good leg as far as the ankle—there it ended in a ragged, oozing mess of trousers and shattered flesh. The man simply sat looking at it. He didn't even stir as we came near, and yet his chest rose and fell with calm breathing, and his mouth was slightly open as if he were day-dreaming. By the side of the ditch knelt another. A soft lead bullet had entered his hand between the two middle fingers and then spread until it hollowed out a bloody cave inside. He had wrapped a rag around a little piece of stick and was unconcernedly dipping it in the water and gouging out the wound.

Soon we were near the battle. In the east, across the vast level country, a faint gray light appeared. . . . It was getting warm, and there came the tranquil smell of earth and grass and growing corn—a calm summer dawn. Into this the noise of battle broke like something insane. The hysterical chatter of rifle fire, that seemed to carry a continuous undertone of screaming—although when you listened for it it was gone. The nervous, deadly stab—stab—stab—stab of the machine guns, like some gigantic woodpecker. The cannon booming like great bells, and the whistle of their shells. Boom—Pi-i-i-e-e-a-uuu! And that most terrible of all the sounds of war, shrapnel exploding. Crash—Whee-e-eaaa!! . . .

The shooting never ceased, but it seemed to be subdued to a subordinate place in a fantastic and disordered world. Up the track in the hot morning light straggled a river of wounded men, shattered, bleeding, bound up in rotting and bloody bandages, inconceivably weary. They passed us, and one even fell and lay motionless nearby in the dust—and we didn't care. Soldiers with their cartridges gone wandered aimlessly out of the chaparral, dragging their rifles, and plunged into the brush again on the other side of the railroad, black with powder, streaked with sweat, their eyes vacantly on the ground. The thin, subtle dust rose in lazy clouds at every footstep, and hung there, parching throat and eyes. A little company of horsemen jogged out of the thicket and drew up on the track, looking toward town. One man got down from his saddle and squatted beside us.

"It was terrible," he said suddenly. ". . . We went in there last night on foot. They were inside the water-tank, with holes cut in the iron for rifles. We had to walk up and poke our guns through the holes and we killed them all—a death trap! And then the Corral! . . . Three thousand *rurales*[1] in there—and they had five machine guns to sweep the road.

---

[1] *rurales*: Rural police.

And the roundhouse, with three rows of trenches outside and subterranean passages so they could crawl under and shoot us in the back. . . . Our bombs wouldn't work, and what could we do with rifles? . . . But we were so quick—we took them by surprise. We captured the roundhouse and the water-tank. And then this morning thousands came—thousands—reinforcements from Torreon—and their artillery—and they drove us back again. They walked up to the water-tank and poked their rifles through the holes and killed all of us—the sons of the devils!"

We could see the place as he spoke and hear the hellish roar and shriek, and yet no one moved, and there wasn't a sign of the shooting—not even smoke, except when a shrapnel shell burst yelling down in the first row of trees a mile ahead and vomited a puff of white. The cracking rip of rifle fire and the staccato machine guns and even the hammering cannon didn't reveal themselves at all. . . .

We returned along the winding path through the mesquite, crossed the torn-up track, and struck out across the dusty plain southeastward. . . . We could see our drab guns rocking down the plain, . . . where the searching fingers of the enemy's shrapnel probed continually. . . .

An old peon, stooped with age and dressed in rags, crouched in the low shrub gathering mesquite twigs.

"Say, friend," we asked him, "is there any way we can get in close to see the fighting?"

He straightened up and stared at us.

"If you had been here as long as I have," said he, "you wouldn't care about seeing the fighting. *Carramba!* I have seen them take Torreon seven times in three years. Sometimes they attack from Gomez Palacio and sometimes from the mountains. But it is always the same—war. There is something interesting in it for the young, but for us old people, we are tired of war." . . . He added incuriously, "What party do you belong to?"

"The Constitutionalists."

"So. First it was the Maderistas, and then the Orozquistas, and now the—what did you call them? I am very old, and I have not long to live; but this war—it seems to me that all it accomplishes is to let us go hungry. Go with God, señores." . . . The shells passing overhead whined sharply and suddenly across the arc of sky and were cut off abruptly until the sullen echoless booff! of their explosion. There ahead, where the railroad trestle of the main line crossed the arroyo, huddled a little pile of bodies—evidently left from the first attack. Hardly one was bloody; their heads and hearts were pierced with the clean, tiny holes of steel Mauser bullets. They lay limply, with the unearthly calm, lean faces of the dead. Someone, perhaps their own thrifty *compañeros*, had stripped them of arms, shoes, hats and serviceable clothing. One sleeping soldier, squatting on the edge of the heap with his rifle across his knees, snored deeply. Flies covered him—the dead hummed with them. But the sun had not yet affected them. Another soldier leaned against the townward bank of the ditch, his feet resting on a corpse, banging methodically away at something he saw. Under the shadow of the trestle four men sat playing cards. They played listlessly, without talking, their eyes red with lack of sleep. The heat was frightful. Occasionally a stray bullet came by screaming, "Where—is-s-s-z—ye!" . . .

. . . About fifty yards in front of us was a shallow exposed ditch, evidently once a Federal trench, for the dirt had been piled on our side. Two hundred drab, dusty soldiers lay in it now, facing townward—the Constitutionalist infantry. They were sprawled on the ground, in all attitudes of weariness; some sleeping on their backs, facing up to the hot sun; others wearily transferring the dirt with their scooped hands from rear to front. Before them they had piled up irregular heaps of rocks. Now infantry, in the Constitutionalist army, is simply cavalry without horses; all Villa's soldiers are mounted except the artillery, and those for whom horses cannot be procured.

Of a sudden the artillery in our rear boomed all together, and over our heads a dozen shells screamed. . . .

"That is the signal," said the man at our side. He clambered down into the ditch and kicked the sleeper. "Come on," he yelled. "Wake up. We're going to attack. . . ." The snorer groaned and opened his eyes slowly. He yawned and picked up his rifle without a word. The card players began to squabble about their winnings. A violent dispute broke out as to who owned the pack of cards. Grumbling and still arguing, they stumbled out and followed the sharpshooter up over the edge of the ditch.

Rifle fire rang along the edge of the trench in front. The sleepers flopped over on their stomachs behind their little shelters—their elbows worked vigorously pumping the guns. The hollow steel water-tank resounded to the rain of thumping bullets. . . . Instantly the wall bristled with shining barrels and the two awoke crackling with hidden vicious firing. Bullets roofed the heavens with whistling steel—drummed the smoking dust up until a yellow curtain of whirling cloud veiled us from the houses and the tank. We could see our friend running low along the ground, the sleepy man following, standing erect, still rubbing his eyes. Behind strung out the gamblers, squabbling yet. Somewhere in the rear a bugle blew. The sharpshooter running in front stopped suddenly, swaying, as if he had run against a solid wall. His left leg doubled under him and he sank crazily to one knee in the exposed flat, whipping up his rifle with a yell.

. . . Now the trench was boiling with men scrambling to their feet, like worms when you turn over a log. The rifle fire rattled shrilly. From behind us came running feet, and men in sandals, with blankets over their shoulders, came falling and slipping down the ditch, and scrambling up the other side—hundreds of them, it seemed. . . .

. . . Suddenly and terribly the monstrous crash and scream of shrapnel burst from the turmoil ahead. The enemy's artillery! Mechanically I listened for our guns. Except for an occasional boom they were silent. Our home-made shells were failing again. Two more shrapnel shells. Out of the dust-cloud men came running back—singly, in pairs, in groups, a stampeding mob. They fell over us, around us—drowned us in a human flood, shouting "To the alamos! To the trains! . . ." We struggled up among them and ran, too, straight up the railroad track. . . . Behind us roared the shells searching in the dust, and the tearing musketry. And then we noticed that all the wide roadway ahead was filled with galloping horsemen, yelling shrill Indian cries and waving their rifles—the main column! We stood to one side as they whirled past, about five hundred of them—watched them stoop in their saddles and begin to shoot. The drumming of their horses' hoofs was like thunder. . . .

I was dead tired, reeling from lack of sleep and food and the terrible heat of the sun. . . . I threw myself down to rest in the shade of a big mesquite bush.

Almost immediately a change seemed to come in the sound of the rifle fire, as if half of it had been suddenly cut off. At the same time twenty bugles shrilled. Rising, I noticed a line of running horsemen fleeing up the track, shouting something. More followed, galloping, at the place where the railroad passed beyond the trees on its way into town. The cavalry had been repulsed. All at once the whole plain squirmed with men, mounted and on foot, all running rearward. . . . The entire Constitutionalist army was routed! I caught up my blanket and took to my heels. A little way farther on I came upon a cannon abandoned in the desert, traces cut, mules gone. Underfoot were guns, cartridge-belts and dozens of serapes. It was a rout. Coming to an open space, I saw ahead a large crowd of fleeing soldiers, without rifles. Suddenly three men on horseback swept across in front of them, waving their arms and yelling. "Go back!" they cried. "They aren't coming out! Go back for the love of God!" Two I didn't recognize. The other was Villa.

11

FRANCISCO "PANCHO" VILLA

The Battle of Tierra Blanca

November 21, 1913

Villa, born Doroteo Arango, rose from obscurity in 1910 to become the head of a formidable army, the Division of the North. That army defeated Victoriano Huerta in 1914 and then went on to fight and lose a series of epic battles to the other great general of the Revolution, Alvaro Obregón in 1915. The Mexican novelist Martín Luis Guzmán maintained that his version of Villa's memoirs, excerpted here, derived from three original memoirs dictated by Villa and written down by different aides. In this selection, the often impulsive Villa shows uncharacteristic patience during the Battle of Tierra Blanca, thirty-five miles south of Ciudad Juárez, where he defeated the army of the counterrevolution led by Huerta. As in the battles to follow, the opposing armies suffered considerable casualties.

That afternoon, November 21, 1913, I ordered a review of my troops, armed, mounted and equipped, for the next morning. At ten they were facing the station. The purpose was not the review. With the brigades assembled and the chiefs present I would give orders to march immediately against the enemy.

I proceeded thus lest I alarm the peaceful people of the town. I wished to keep the frontier quiet and protect international business. Furthermore, it was desirable to keep my preparations a secret from the enemy. Knowing they were on the march I let them advance in order to meet them at a place I had chosen, the plain stretching from Bauche station to Tierra Blanca, where I would occupy a position on the high ground, leaving them a sandy tract to immobilize their artillery and slow their other movements. They would have no water there or way of getting it. . . .

I left Juárez at ten in the morning with 6,200 men. At Mesa I called a council of my brigade chiefs and gave them instructions. . . .

From Martín Luis Guzmán, *Memoirs of Pancho Villa*, trans. Virginia H. Taylor (Austin: University of Texas Press, 1965), 118–22.

I said, "Amigos, this battle determines the future of the Revolution. If we are defeated, we lose Juárez and the frontier, with access to arms and ammunition. We must win."

That same afternoon we saw the enemy trains four kilometers from our positions. According to my calculations there were some 5,500 men of the three branches, and the famous cannons called "El Rorro" and "El Chavalito" on their platforms. . . .

Thus passed the night of the twenty-second. In the morning I was expecting them to attack, but either because of the heavy mist or for other reasons, they stayed quietly in their positions, and we let them see we were waiting in ours. We faced each other like that for several hours. . . .

The battle began the next morning at five. My right wing, which [Maclovio] Herrera and Eugenio Aguirre Benavides were covering, met the attack of [Manuel] Landa and [Marcelo] Caraveo's cavalry. The enemy thought they could easily crumple that flank, when my center would soon give way. To let them know that a movement against any single point of my line would provoke an assault, I threw my center into action, and, seeing that they left their line uncovered on the west and only infantry protected their trains on the east, I ordered an advance. My center moved. Porfirio Talamantes, at the cost of his life, got up to the first enemy engine with part of the reserves. But the fire from the sandbanks at the right of their line caused many casualties. I ordered my line to retire, for my purpose, already accomplished, had been only to relieve my right wing. Besides, I wanted to see if, encouraged by my retreat, their infantry would abandon the only natural defenses I had left them.

They did not fall into the trap; they stayed sheltered as they were. Seeing that their two large cannon were attempting to advance, I ordered [Martiniano] Servín's artillery to stop them, and he not only did so but drove them back. Now, with control of the center, I ordered Fidel Avila to take four hundred of the Villa Brigade horses and go to the aid of Herrera and Aguirre Benavides. We were frustrating Landa and Caraveo in their efforts to gain control of Bauche, which they desperately needed for the water tanks there. At eleven that morning Herrera, Aguirre Benavides, and Avila pushed them back to the trains, causing many casualties and taking many prisoners.

Meanwhile, [José Inés] Salazar and [Rafael] Flores Alatorre on my left were trying to break through the lines held by Rosalío Hernández and José Rodríguez. Their strength was great, and such was their determination that they upset my two brigades. But recovering their balance, my men cut off part of Salazar's troops, and as Hernández pursued and annihilated these, the main body of Salazar's forces withdrew in disorder, saved only by the protection of a cloud of dust on the Zaragoza road.

During the action I received supplies and other necessaries from Ciudad Juárez. Trains arrived with water, bread, and fodder, as well as ammunition and machine guns. Private automobiles from Juárez and El Paso brought medicine and nurses. The wounded who were strong enough I put on trains and sent to Ciudad Juárez. There were many, and the mortality was great. . . .

Daybreak on the twenty-fifth found Flores Alatorre's forces strong in their right-wing positions but far from their purpose of routing my left. The fighting spread. It increased on the line defended by Rodríguez and Hernández. The opposing forces were beginning to paralyze Rodríguez' movements when, obeying my orders, he advanced with all the daring of a Revolutionary. But he fell wounded, and Flores Alatorre, who had received reinforcements, charged and began to force us back to the Hippodrome.

Seeing that my left was being overwhelmed and that this threatened my whole position, I sent word to General [Toribio] Ortega and to Avila and other officers all along the line to order a general cavalry attack on the signal of two cannon shots; to give this signal I waited only for the moment that would ensure the success of the charge.

As I waited, Herrera came and asked what he was to do, since the enemy were almost crushing him. I answered, "On the signal all the cavalry will fall on the enemy. Have confidence, Señor. Do what we are all going to do, move forward, crowd them back against their trains, and annihilate them."

So it turned out. At the signal we fell on them with such fury that we had them defeated at every point before they could recover their balance. We caught them with their artillery bogged in the sand at a time when their infantry had left the protection of ridges. Their panic was so great that some tried to run, others tumbled into the sand, and hardly a one faced us or remembered to use his arms. We wounded or killed them with our pistols, and there were no less than two hundred casualties. We took many prisoners and several of their cannon. The entire enemy line was broken and at the mercy of my center, which had broken through toward the east and west as my two wings were closing in and forcing them to scatter.

At nightfall we attacked the trains. . . . Rodolfo Fierro, at the head of the Corps of Scouts, ran his horse at full gallop to overtake a trainload who were escaping. In a rain of bullets he leaped from his horse to the train and climbing from one car to another reached the brake cylinder, released the air, and stopped the train. . . . Soldiers from the Corps of Scouts and my brigade then fell on the train, and the slaughter was horrible.

The battle of Tierra Blanca, according to my memory, began on November 23, 1913, and ended two days later at night. The enemy lost more than one thousand men and left me three trains and two pieces of artillery.

12

J. B. TREVIÑO

A Losing General's Perspective

ca. 1916

Although Obregón destroyed Villa's army in 1915, the former bandit remained a formidable force in northern Mexico, especially Chihuahua. Venustiano Carranza's army could not end Villa's resistance. In this dispatch, General J. B. Treviño, who headed the army sent by Carranza to stop Villa in 1916, describes a difficult few days. He blames others for his defeat, extols the bravery of his soldiers, and defends his own honor. Treviño, educated at Mexico's national military college as an engineer, was one of the best-trained officers in any of the revolutionary armies. He refers to his foes as "bandits," clearly indicating his disdain for them. Indeed, there was much bitterness between the Carrancistas and the Villistas.

To: General Alvaro Obregón
From: J. B. Treviño

Permit me to communicate with you that on the 27th at 3 a.m. the bandits initiated a desperate attack over the whole area and after two hours, having completely exhausted our ammunition, I was obligated to withdraw our forces which we effected in relative order, part of our cavalry and infantry leaving on trains going north and another part of the same with the undersigned to Aldama. This last I did with the object of

From J. B. Treviño to Alvaro Obregón, dispatch, no date, in Friedrich Katz, "La Última Gran Campaña de Francisco Villa," *Boletín* (Fideicomiso Archivos Plutarco Elías Calles y Fernando Torreblanca), no. 5 (1991). Translated by Mark Wasserman.

looking to link with the column of General Murguía, which did not take place until the 30th in the Bachimba station, from where he continued the advance of said column encountering the enemy between Horca-sitas station and the Masula station on the 1st of the present month. Earlier I fought six hours, myself taking direct command of the infantry and which combat resulted disastrously for the bandits, who fled in different directions, with the main body of them heading to Santa Isabel. Yesterday, the advance continued to this plaza, which was abandoned by the enemy, General Murguía's column taking possession of it at 7 p.m. The bandits had set out to sack the town and shoot the municipal president and some civilians. During the four days of the defense of this plaza, it took great force to save it, but the effort was futile because of the complete scarcity of munitions, . . . The soldiers who defended this plaza endured defeat that deserves the honorable opinion of this city. . . . All of my officers did their duty and as a result the majority were killed or wounded. I consider myself to have complied with my duty to the very end. Having been wounded in this action, I ask respectfully that you permit me to travel to the capital of the Republic to attend to reestablishing my health. Advise me the best method by which I can deliver the forces under my command.

13

EMILIANO ZAPATA

The Possibility of Alliance with Villa

1914

In this letter, written January 19, 1914 at the height of Villa's military power, Zapata, deeply disillusioned by the reluctance of Madero and Carranza to endorse the immediate redistribution of land in Morelos and other regions, probes for common ground to form an alliance with Villa. Later in 1914, Villa and Zapata would join together to capture Mexico City. But theirs was an ambivalent partnership. In 1915, Zapata would

From Emiliano Zapata to Francisco Villa, January 19, 1914, in Richard M. Estrada, "Zapata to Villa, Revolutionary Camp in Morelos, January 19, 1914," *Proceedings of the Pacific Coast Council on Latin American Studies* 8 (1981–1982): 165–67.

not commit his forces to assist Villa against Carranza, accounting at
least in part for Villa's defeat.

The Liberating Army of the South and Center

General Francisco Villa
Ciudad Juárez, Chihuahua

Esteemed General and friend:
   I received yours dated November 28, 1913, which I have read closely
and I respond to you that the ideals of the Revolution of the South and
Center of the Republic have always been and will continue to be those
of "Land and Liberty"; that they are the hopes and ardent desires of the
Mexican people, and even though it is true as you say that our enemies
intrigue toward the end of undermining the noble and just cause that we
defend, they will never be successful while there remains one human
being alive in these regions of our nation; and rest assured that we, the
southern revolutionaries, will not allow ourselves to be deceived, for
the war of three long years has provided us with hard lessons, and I
await [the expression of a] similar position from you, [i.e.] that you will
not allow the traitors and false supporters of the revolutionary cause
to deceive you. Remember the case of Pascual Orozco, Jr., who, after
distinguishing himself for his patriotism and good intentions in favor of
the fatherland, to the point of occupying a respected place in the history
of our country, turned his arms against the fatherland and established
a common cause with those who betrayed it, and there you have him!
Defending the interests of the enemies of progress and well-being of the
Republic. Damned by all who believe they have the right to call themselves Mexicans, and why? Because he allowed himself to be deceived by
our enemies. And therefore I say to you, and as you similarly expressed
to me, that we not let ourselves be deceived by our enemies. Let us be
wary of those false idealists, who eventually turn into fanatical personalists, let us beware of those personalists who masked as idealists proceed
to ruin the fatherland[.] As you well know by experience . . . the person-
alist causes have never brought happiness to the nation, but on the contrary, those causes always were, are, and will be the misfortune of the
Republic; there is our history, as if the sad events of three long years of
war were not enough to demonstrate it. Because of that I repeat to you,
that we should be vigilant of all our companions and false supporters so
that we will not be surprised, and so that our cause will not be betrayed
and the people's will not be mocked.

You tell me in your aforementioned letter, which I am pleased to answer, that the day is not far off when we will have to attack the capital of the Republic with blood and fire, sweeping away all of those corrupt elements who are the enemies of the people, who are called científicos, militarism and clericalism[.] . . . The truth is: . . . we have to undertake these executions in order to finish off these enemies of the fatherland, because only in that manner will there be peace and will the reforms of the Revolution be put into effect. Remember that the Revolution which began on November 20, 1910 failed solely because upon entering Mexico City it did not decapitate its enemies, and they were the ones who ultimately defeated it. . . .

Believe me, that I like my comrades, the southern revolutionaries, have always had faith in the triumph of our cause, not just now that the evil and illegal government is moribund, but rather, ever since the South continued the Revolution, begun by Madero, when he took possession of the presidential chair and betrayed the people; when only the South raised the standard of liberty, justice and law, where its sons, boldly and courageously combatted the treacherous Government; when the idealistic Government, which turned into a personalistic and dictatorial government, counted on adequate forces with which to fight us.

I am similarly impressed that *you are about to take the capital of the State of Chihuahua, and that afterwards you will begin the division of the lands among the people, beginning by dividing those lands that are in possession of the enemy,* and with regard to this matter, I must say to you that it is to be hoped that this division of lands will be effected in accordance with the stipulations of the Plan de Ayala, which in its relevant part states these words:

> Sixth.—As an additional part of the plan we invoke, we give notice: that [regarding] the fields, timber, and water which the landlords, cientificos or bosses have usurped, the pueblos or citizens who have titles corresponding to those properties will immediately enter into possession of that real estate of which they have been despoiled by the bad faith of our oppressors, maintaining at any cost with arms in hand the mentioned possession; and the usurpers who consider themselves with a right to them (those properties) will deduce it before the special tribunals which will be established on the triumph of the revolution.

And, lastly, I assure you that if the villages are given what belongs to them and if the Plan de Ayala is complied with, the peace of the nation will be assured and the prosperity and well-being of the Republic will be a fact.

Similarly, I hope that I will soon be able to embrace you and that you will soon approach the capital of the Republic, so that we may be in contact and plan the triumphal entry into Mexico City, and then yes, the Revolution will hoist the flag of reform, liberty, justice and law over the National Palace.

Without further [thoughts] for the moment, and . . . [repeating my desire] that you not forget my recommendation that the partitioning of lands in the North be undertaken in conformity with the Plan of Ayala—because I have faith that you may well be the only one in the North who is concerned with the progress of the people, and the one who essays to effect in those regions the division of lands and the parcelling of the large monopolies of lands, as is indicated by the Plan de Ayala—, I salute you and your comrades-in-arms, to whom I hope you will convey my respects.

I am your most affectionate, attentive and faithful friend and servant.

EL GENERAL
[Emiliano Zapata]

14

ALVARO OBREGÓN

The Battle at Celaya

April 13–15, 1915

Alvaro Obregón was indisputably the best general of the Revolution. More than his mortal enemy, Pancho Villa, he adapted his tactics to modern warfare, using trenches, barbed wire, and machine guns to frustrate the daring and ultimately failed attacks of his opponent. A Sonoran, he joined the Revolution late in 1911, later attaching himself to Venustiano Carranza after the death of Francisco Madero in 1913. He defeated Villa in a series of hard-fought battles in the spring of 1915. During one of those battles, he lost an arm. Bleeding profusely from his wound, he tried unsuccessfully to kill himself, only to have the gun jam. Obregón was elected president in 1920 and served until 1924. He fell victim to an assassin's bullet in 1928, just after his election for a second term as

From Alvaro Obregón, *Ocho Mil Kilometros en Campaña* (1917; repr., Mexico City: Fondo de Cultura Económica, 1959), 311–14. Translated by Mark Wasserman.

president. His memoir, Ocho Mil Kilometros en Campaña *(*Eight Thousand Miles in Campaign *), primarily describes his military campaigns against Huerta's federal army in 1913 and 1914. This selection, however, is about the crucial battle against Villa's forces at Celaya in 1915, when Obregón used Villa's impatience to defeat him.*

At five in the afternoon the battle begins. Initially, we heard fire from the front of the positions occupied by the First Brigade of Infantry, which ended after a short while. At six our side opened fire, the artillery began, and in a few minutes, bombardments erupted from all of the cannon from both sides. By nine at night the hard-fought battle spread over a zone of approximately twelve kilometers.

The enemy continued to advance on our flanks, then attacked our rear guard. . . . The reactionaries continued to attack and suffered large losses.

The artillery did not cease. The assaults continued through breakfast on the fourteenth. Protected by the night, the enemy advanced to within five hundred meters of our lines. The land was perfectly flat and deforested, and there was no hiding the combatants, who fought desperately. Our troops did not retreat a single step, and the enemy did not succeed in taking any of our positions. At five a.m. I ordered reinforcements. . . . And the fighting continued until dusk.

In the morning there occurred a bloody battle on our flanks. . . . I ordered my troops to continue the fight until 7 a.m. the next day, when the cavalry would attack the enemy flanks. . . . All replied that the spirits of the troops were high and that they would continue to fight in these conditions. . . .

At noon I had a telegraphic conference with General Cesáreo Castro, manifesting my wishes to shift the burden to the cavalry the next day, at which time the enemy, without noticing our movements, would believe us lost and then commit his reserves into the line of fire and result in a complete disaster. The battle continued with bloodshed at the flanks and center. . . .

After four a.m. on the fifteenth I ordered General Amaro and others to involve their troops to the right of the enemy, where the reactionaries amounted to 6,000 and had taken position on the banks of the Río La Laja.

On the morning of the 15th I ordered General Hill's infantry, then acting as a defensive line on the right flank, in support of the cavalry column on the right of the enemy. . . . I ordered General Laveaza to cover the right flank. . . . The cavalry dislocated the enemy at the Hacienda de Higueras; after an hour of combat they advanced to the Hacienda de Burgos. Although the enemy had unprecedented numbers . . . we vigorously attacked the front and left flank. Our infantry dispersed in the wheat fields, continuing decisively, its advance throwing them over the lines occupied by the enemy, and one by one they took the positions of the enemy, despite the useless desperation of the reactionaries. Meanwhile, the cavalry had begun to take Villista prisoners.

3

Soldiers' Lives

We will never know how many soldiers and civilians died in the Revolution. The evidence we have indicates that the population declined by one million to two million people, but these were not all casualties of the fighting. Many thousands fled across the northern border and were untraceable thereafter. Others may have died in the Spanish influenza pandemic of 1918. It is estimated that 1.5 million Mexicans (10 percent of the population), men and women, were under arms during the decade-long wars. At the height of the fighting in 1915, there were 150,000 soldiers in both the Constitutionalist (Carranza and Obregón) and the Conventionalist (Villa and Zapata) armies.

Historians have not written extensively about the lives of soldiers during the Revolution. The best insights we have often come from contemporary reporters and novelists. Aside from a few officers trained in the national military school, the leaders of the Revolution learned about strategy, tactics, logistics, and management as they went along. The troops were often undisciplined and unreliable, and desertion was a constant problem. The soldiers' lives were harsh, for they were frequently short on rations and ammunition and did not have proper shelter or clothing. As in all wars, keeping the armies fed and armed was crucial.

15

JOHN REED

The Soldaderas

1914

This selection from Reed's Insurgent Mexico *illustrates the essential role of women in the Revolution and the relentless horror of war. Indeed, Elizabetta showed remarkable courage and resilience. A refugee from a war-torn village, she had gone off to war involuntarily; it was the only way for her to survive. Like so many other* soldaderas, *she was often treated badly, but she persevered. And like her sisters in arms on all sides, she was indispensable to the war effort.*

It was not yet quite dark. I wandered . . . in the vague hope of finding some of my *compadres* who were still reported missing. And it was there that I first saw Elizabetta.

There was nothing remarkable about her. I think I noticed her chiefly because she was one of the few women in that wretched company. She was a very dark-skinned Indian girl, about twenty-five years old, with the squat figure of her drudging race, pleasant features, hair hanging forward over her shoulders in two long plaits, and big, shining teeth when she smiled. . . .

Now she was trudging stolidly along in the dust behind Captain Felix Romero's horse—and had trudged so for thirty miles. He never spoke to her, never looked back, but rode on unconcernedly. Sometimes he would get tired of carrying his rifle and hand it back to her to carry, with a careless "Here! Take this!" I found out later that when they returned to La Cadena after the battle to bury the dead he had found her wandering aimlessly in the hacienda, apparently out of her mind; and that, needing a woman, he had ordered her to follow him. Which she did, unquestioningly, after the custom of her sex and country.

Captain Felix let his horse drink. Elizabetta halted, too, knelt and plunged her face into the water.

From John Reed, *Insurgent Mexico* (New York: Appleton, 1914), 103–9, 196–98.

"Come on," ordered the Captain. "*Andale!*" She rose without a word and waded through the stream. In the same order they climbed the near bank, and there the Captain dismounted, held out his hand for the rifle she carried, and said, "Get me my supper!" Then he strolled away toward the houses where the rest of the soldiers sat.

Elizabetta fell upon her knees and gathered twigs for her fire. Soon there was a little pile burning. She called a small boy in the harsh, whining voice that all Mexican women have, "*Aei! chamaco!*[1] Fetch me a little water and corn that I may feed my man!" And, rising upon her knees above the red glow of the flames, she shook down her long, straight black hair. She wore a sort of blouse of faded light blue rough cloth. There was dried blood on the breast of it.

"What a battle, señorita!" I said to her.

Her teeth flashed as she smiled, and yet there was a puzzling vacancy about her expression. Indians have mask-like faces. Under it I could see that she was desperately tired and even a little hysterical. But she spoke tranquilly enough.

"Perfectly," she said. "Are you the Gringo who ran so many miles with the *colorados* after you shooting?" And she laughed—catching her breath in the middle of it as if it hurt.

The *chamaco* shambled up with an earthen jar of water and an armful of corn-ears that he tumbled at her feet. Elizabetta unwound from her shawl the heavy little stone trough that Mexican women carry, and began mechanically husking the corn into it.

"I do not remember seeing you at La Cadena," I said. "Were you there long?"

"Too long," she answered simply, without raising her head. And then suddenly, "Oh, but this war is no game for women!" she cried.

Don Felix loomed up out of the dark, with a cigarette in his mouth.

"My dinner," he growled. "Is it *pronto*?"

"*Luego, luego!*" she answered. He went away again.

"Listen, señor, whoever you are!" said Elizabetta swiftly, looking up to me. "My lover was killed yesterday in the battle. This man is my man, but, by God and all the Saints, I can't sleep with him this night. Let me stay then with you!"

There wasn't a trace of coquetry in her voice. This blundering, childish spirit had found itself in a situation it couldn't bear, and had chosen the instinctive way out. I doubt if she even knew herself why the thought

---

[1] *chamaco*: Kid.

of this new man so revolted her, with her lover scarcely cold in the ground. I was nothing to her, nor she to me. That was all that mattered.

I assented, and together we left the fire, the Captain's neglected corn spilling from the stone trough. And then we met him a few feet into the darkness.

"My dinner!" he said impatiently. His voice changed. "Where are you going?"

"I'm going with this señor," Elizabetta answered nervously. "I'm going to stay with him—"

"You—" began Don Felix, gulping. "You are my woman. *Oiga*, señor, this is my woman here!"

"Yes," I said. "She is your woman. I have nothing to do with her. But she is very tired and not well, and I have offered her my bed for the night."

"This is very bad, señor!" exclaimed the Captain, in a tightening voice. "You are the guest of this Tropa and the Colonel's friend, but this is my woman and I want her—"

"Oh!" Elizabetta cried out. "Until the next time, señor!" She caught my arm and pulled me on.

We had been living in a nightmare of battle and death—all of us. I think everybody was a little dazed and excited. I know I was.

By this time the peons and soldiers had begun to gather around us, and as we went on the Captain's voice rose as he retailed his injustice to the crowd.

"I shall appeal to the Colonel," he was saying. "I shall tell the Colonel!" He passed us, going toward the Colonel's cuartel, with averted, mumbling face.

"*Oiga, mi Coronel!*" he cried. "This Gringo has taken away my woman. It is the grossest insult!"

"Well," returned the Colonel calmly, "if they both want to go, I guess there isn't anything we can do about it, eh?" . . .

Without the least embarrassment, Elizabetta lay down beside me on the bed. Her hand reached for mine. She snuggled against my body for the comforting human warmth of it, murmured, "Until morning," and went to sleep. And calmly, sweetly, sleep came to me. . . .

When I woke in the morning she was gone. I opened my door and looked out. . . .

Elizabetta was squatted over a little fire near the corner of the house, patting *tortillas* for the Captain's breakfast. She smiled as I came up, and politely asked me if I had slept well. She was quite contented now; you knew from the way she sang over her work.

Presently the Captain came up in a surly manner and nodded briefly to me.

"I hope it's ready now," he grunted, taking the *tortillas* she gave him. "You take a long time to cook a little breakfast. *Carramba!* Why is there no coffee?" He moved off, munching. "Get ready," he flung back over his shoulder. "We go north in an hour."

"Are you going?" I asked curiously. Elizabetta looked at me with wide-open eyes.

"Of course I am going. *Seguro!* Is he not my man?" She looked after him admiringly. She was no longer revolted.

"He is my man," she said. "He is very handsome, and very brave. Why, in the battle the other day—"

Elizabetta had forgotten her lover. . . .

About two o'clock in the morning I came upon two *soldaderas* squatting around a fire, and asked them if they could give me *tortillas* and coffee. One was an old, gray-haired Indian woman with a perpetual grin, the other a slight girl not more than twenty years old, who was nursing a four-months baby at her breast. They were perched at the extreme tip of a flat-car, their fire built upon a pile of sand, as the train jolted and swayed along. Around them, backed against them, feet sticking out between them, was a great, inconglomerate mass of sleeping, snoring humans. The rest of the train was by this time dark; this was the only patch of light and warmth in the night. As I munched my *tortilla* and the old woman lifted a burning coal in her fingers to light her corn-husk cigarette, wondering where her Pablo's brigade was this night; and the girl nursed her child, crooning to it, her blue-enameled earrings twinkling, —we talked.

"Ah! it is a life for us *viejas*," said the girl. "*Adio*, but we follow our men out in the campaign, and then do not know from hour to hour whether they live or die. I remember well when Filadelfo called to me one morning in the little morning before it was light—we lived in Pachuca—and said: 'Come! we are going out to fight because the good Pancho Madero has been murdered this day!' We had only been loving each other eight months, too, and the first baby was not born. . . . We had all believed that peace was in Mexico for good. Filadelfo saddled the burro, and we rode out through the streets just as light was coming, and into the fields where the farmers were not yet at work. And I said: 'Why must I come?' And he answered: 'Shall I starve, then? Who shall make my *tortillas* for me but my woman?' It took us three months to get north, and I was sick and the baby was born in a desert just like this place, and died there because we could not get water. That was when Villa was going north after he had taken Torreon."

The old woman broke in: "Yes, and all that is true. When we go so far and suffer so much for our men, we are cruelly treated by the stupid animals of Generals. I am from San Luis Potosi, and my man was in the artillery of the Federacion when Mercado came north. All the way to Chihuahua we traveled, the old fool of a Mercado grumbling about transporting the *viejas*. And then he ordered his army to go north and attack Villa in Juarez, and he forbade the women to go. Is that the way you are going to do, *desgraciado*? I said to myself. And when he evacuated Chihuahua and ran away with my man to Ojinaga, I just stayed right in Chihuahua and got a man in the Maderista army when it came in. A nice handsome young fellow, too,—much better than Juan. I'm not a woman to stand being put upon."

16

ANTHONY QUINN

A Soldier's Wife

1972

The Mexican-born American movie star and Academy Award winner Anthony Quinn's autobiography includes his beloved mother Manuela's account of her participation in the Revolution as a soldadera *between 1913 and 1915. His father, Francisco, met his mother when they were teenagers, ages seventeen and fifteen, respectively. Francisco was the blond son of an Irishman. His widowed mother had a pension from the railroad and was consequently middle-class. Manuela was from a very poor family. Immediately after they met, they went off to join the army. Their story seems romantic, but it also informs us of the circumstances of women in the Revolution and the importance of young people in the ranks of all the factions.*

"One day the boy, his name was Francisco, came up to me. It was a Saturday afternoon, and he said, 'I am going to join the army and I want you to be my soldadera.'

From Anthony Quinn, *The Original Sin: A Self-Portrait* (Boston: Little, Brown, 1972), 26–30.

"Of course I was astounded. Imagine the nerve! 'Why?' I asked.

"'Because I believe in the revolution and Pancho Villa.'

"'No,' I said. 'Why do you want me to be your soldadera? You hardly know me.'

"'I've seen you around, and I like you, and well. . . .' He looked off into space as if he was annoyed that I wanted any explanation. 'Anyway, I decided that if I went off to fight I would like you beside me, that's all.'

"Funny, but something about the way he said it, seemed to say so much more—and he was handsome. 'I'll think about it,' I said. And I walked away.

"That night I couldn't get that boy out of my mind. There was something lonely, wild and strange about him. A few days later, when I was coming out of the bakery, he was standing there, as if he was still waiting for my answer.

"'Well?' he said. . . .

"'A train is leaving tomorrow to join Villa down south. I'm going to be on it. They say it leaves at dawn.' And he walked away.

"That night I bundled a few of my things.

"At dawn I left the house.

"The station was filled with young men and women. There was almost a festive air, as if we were all going to a picnic instead of a war.

"I looked around for Francisco. Finally, I saw him in his big sombrero and with bandoleros across his chest. He towered over the rest. I ran toward him. I had hoped my appearance would finally make him break down and say something nice, something romantic. Instead he said, 'So you decided to come?'

"What could I say, but 'Yes, I want to fight for the revolution.'

"He smiled as if one excuse was as good as the other. 'Okay, come on.'

"He led me to one of the freight cars that were to carry us south to Durango. I followed him as if I'd been walking behind him forever. We'd never even held hands.

"As the train chugged through the brown countryside, everyone in the freight car was singing songs. Men sat in groups around other men playing their guitars. The women sat around cleaning guns or sewing. Francisco and I sat against the front end of the car. We were more protected there from the wind that came through the wide-open slats.

"We hadn't spoken much. He stared out at the speeding countryside most of the time.

"Around noon the train came to a halt in the middle of the desert. We were all ordered to get off the train. The women were told to feed their men. All the women made a dash for the fields, where we gathered dried mesquite to build our fires. Thank God my mother had taught me to cook, so I didn't disgrace myself among the other women.

"Francisco said the tacos were very good. He even invited a couple of the other men who didn't have their women with them. They all complimented him on his woman's cooking. He just nodded.

"After a while we were speeding south again. The sun was going down behind the mountains and the air was getting cold. People started covering themselves with their rebozos and serapes. A few lit kerosene lamps. In the car someone was singing softly and other people were preparing to go to sleep.

"It occurred to me that soon I would have to do the same. I would have to go to sleep near this boy whom I hardly knew, this boy who had never said pretty things to me and who just took me for granted.

"He saw me shivering there in the cold. 'Come on, get under the blanket.'

"I said, 'I can't sleep with you.'

"'That's crazy. I'm not going to touch you. Just get under the covers. It's cold.'

"I shook my head.

"'You think people can only sleep together when they are married?' he laughed.

"'Of course,' I said, knowing that it wasn't true.

"At the other end of the car was a priest.

"Francisco called to him, 'Father, come over here. This girl and I want to be married.'

"The priest was a very young man. I don't think he'd ever performed the marriage ceremony before.

"'Well, I don't know . . . ,' he said.

"Francisco became annoyed. 'Look, we're in a war and this train could be dynamited any second. This girl and I want to be married before we die.'

"The first thing Francisco said after the simple rites was, 'All right, get under the blanket.'

"A few days later we reached Durango and got off the train and made camp.

"Next day a sergeant came up and ordered all the men to pick up their guns and follow him. Francisco picked up his gear with all the rest and they started up a hill where we could hear shooting.

"We women just stood there and watched our men march off to their first battle. Many of the men looked back and waved to their women. Francisco never did.

"The horror of the war for me was the waiting. We women waited there all night, listening to the shooting. I found myself kneeling. I prayed he would come through that first battle.

"Next morning at dawn a horseman came and told us to pick up our blankets and food and go and cook for our men.

"From the top of the hill I saw what a battle meant. There were bodies all over the plain. Some were dead, some were wounded. Many were asleep, exhausted from the fighting of the night before.

"You could hear the screams of women as they discovered their men dead or wounded.

"Finally, I heard a voice: 'Manuela!' There he was sitting behind a rock. That was the first time he'd called me by name.

"As I walked toward him I could see a new look in his eyes. 'Manuela, it was great. It was better than I had expected. I was afraid I'd be scared, but when the shooting started I wasn't afraid at all.' He didn't say he was glad to see me.

"I knelt beside him and cooked him his breakfast. He could hardly eat, he was so excited at what had happened the night before.

"I understood so much about him that day. He was different from the rest of the men. To them he was a 'gringo'—his name was Quinn. He was always trying to prove that he was as Mexican as they were. Later I saw him get in many fights in camp because someone would make the mistake of calling him 'gringo.' Here he was fighting for the revolution, and his own comrades would not accept him as one of them.

"After that first battle, one was like the other. The same smell of gunpowder, the same sounds of the bugle, the shooting and the cries of the wounded. The same fears at the end of each battle that he would not return.

"I don't know if I was in love with him. One didn't have time to ask such questions.

"Those first few battles had changed all my girlish ideas of love. We were not characters in a fairy tale. I wasn't waiting for my knight to come on a white charger. I was constantly afraid that the next charger would be black and that he would take my man.

"Love was ugly hours of waiting and fears. Love was cooking for your man as he went off to battle, mending his clothes when he returned. Love was giving thanks to God that your man was still alive.

"One night, a few months later while we were all packed down on the train—this time shuttled farther south to Zacatecas—I told him I had felt the first stirrings of you in my belly. He laughed.

"A few days later, we women were washing clothes on a riverbank when a sergeant rode up. 'Any of you women pregnant?'

"A few of us held up our hands, and we were told to go to camp and gather up our belongings. We were being sent back to our homes because they felt the men didn't fight as well when they had to worry about their pregnant women.

"We begged the sergeant to let us say good-bye to our men. He refused. Some of us were carried bodily and put on the train leaving for Chihuahua. I cried for the first time at being separated from Francisco. I realized that I *was* his woman. I wondered who would feed him, who would take care of him."

17

VETERANS OF THE MEXICAN REVOLUTION

Experiences of the War

1910–1920

By some estimates, nearly a million Mexicans may have emigrated to the United States during the Mexican Revolution. Many who left were veterans of the fighting. They remained silent about their experiences for decades. In the 1970s, however, there was a movement to tell their stories. One group in California, Veterans of the Mexican Revolution, established an oral history project with U.S. government funding. Excerpts from three of the interviews follow.

Jesús Avila went to war when he was fifteen, drafted into Villa's army. It did not matter that his uncle and father were influential men; he could not escape conscription. Avila came of age in the gory battles of the Revolution. Nicolás Durán fought under a general who remained loyal to Villa even after his defeats in 1915. His band of soldiers sought to continue the fight as others left the army and returned home. Durán expresses special appreciation of the women who fought alongside their men. Maria Villasana López left her village involuntarily, dragged off to war by a general in Carranza's army. When he was killed, she and her daughter struggled to survive.

From Esther R. Pérez, James Kallas, and Nina Kallas, eds., *Those Years of the Revolution, 1910–1920: Authentic Bilingual Life Experiences as Told by the Veterans of the War* (San Jose, Calif.: Aztlán Today, 1974), 145–47, 155–57, 208.

Jesús Avila

Colonel Ornelas was under Villa's command. He was also my uncle. Ornelas and his soldiers became Carrancistas and refused to further take orders from Villa. Villa took Ornelas and imprisoned him. His plans were to execute Ornelas for defecting to the Carrancistas. My father then counteracted Villa's order and had Ornelas freed and taken to Texas for protection. It was then that my father and brother became Villa's enemies. My father secretly left the country for Texas. Once in Texas he sent orders that my brother and I were to join him. Confused, frightened and unsure, we rushed to the office of immigration for our necessary papers. To our dismay and fear we found that we were being followed by Villa's soldiers. Unfortunately, the office was closed. Guadalupe, my brother, thought that we should head for my grandparent's home which was located on the Terrazas brothers' land. Running scared and hiding like hunted men we traveled through the Sierras until we reached Tierra Blanca. We spent another five days in the wilderness merely trying to survive. Our journey was thought to be ended when we reached the Hacienda. Upon arrival we were informed that to stay there would be too dangerous so we moved on to a cattle ranch called La Gotera. The ranch was a sanctuary for my brother and I. The life on the ranch along with my frustrations caused me to leave. I was only fourteen but I did not fear going back to my grandfather's house. . . .

Sometime later Villa issued a decree in the State of Chihuahua. Every male member of a family was to serve in his troops. At that particular time I was at my grandfather's home. I was barely fifteen years old but still I was chosen along with my uncle to serve. My grandfather was too old and so he remained behind. My brother and I were taken to a fort and were trained for the course of one week. After a week's time we were given arms and told to attack General Murgia who was in the process of taking three of Carranza's trains in the North.

We planned to take by surprise the train station at Horcacitas. Much to our surprise the infantry was hiding under the trains, ready for us. Many of our men were killed but my brother and I luckily escaped to the hills. We were happy to find that near our hiding place was General Modesto Balderrama. He was once a Colonel under my father's command. We stayed close by his side. After a week of fighting the opposition Balderrama was killed. He was shot like so many of our men, but this shot seemed to even wound me, internally from my heart. It was heartless and so ugly the way the men fought over his clothes. Soon after Balderrama's death I lost my brother. He was gone. In my platoon only five hundred men remained. The General was dead and we were in desperate need of a replacement. General Marin Lopez was a brave man but he usually went into a battle in a drunken stupor. I, myself, did not let this uncaring attitude affect me. I fought with such fervor and strength that whenever I fired a shot I rarely missed. I was proud of this. A young man needs something to be proud of so that he might continue to go on even under such hardships. My horse was my pride and joy. It was a jewel of an animal and I treasured it. I trained him to defend me in battle. As I was busy firing I saw another man trying to take my horse. Forgetting my age and who I was, I rushed to him and ordered that he leave my horse alone or I would kill him. Imagine killing a man for a horse. The man to my amazement obeyed me. It was at that time that I realized the potential a gun has in the hand of a person whether they be but a young boy or a man. . . .

A few days later I was somewhat overjoyed because my brother was found and had returned. Immediately following his return we were ordered by Villa to return to the battle lines. Our new mission was to overtake the city of Chihuahua. At this time both of us were concerned about our father. He knew nothing of what happened to us and we had no means by which to meet him in Texas. The overall situation seemed hopeless. Our battalion received orders to stay outside the City. We were not getting very far for every time our reinforcements arrived the enemy would get them first.

Our men were being killed in masses. We were all huddled in the ground like nesting birds trying to keep warm. We were told not to move or get up. I could hear sounds; cries, gunshots and at times still-ness. My curiosity was building up and building up. I couldn't tolerate lying there any longer. I stood up so that I could see what was really going on. Dear God, what a sight. Hundreds and hundreds of lifeless men lay there. Blood was everywhere as if it had fallen from the sky like rain. A head there, a hand over there. Dismangled trunks of a onetime person. It looked like a junk yard for body parts. Some died looking upward while others died facing the blood strewn earth. Some were curled up in a fetal position and some were nothing at all. . . .

Hours later the remaining troops began to clean the battle field of the onetime life that it supported. Dozens upon dozens of carts loaded with bodies passed me by and I just stood there. I could hear many still crying out. I hated, I condemned, I cursed, and I vowed until my heart was so full of pity and sadness that it was ready to burst. It was at that time that I swore to myself and to all those dead bodies that I would never touch another pistol again. I pointed my rifle to the ground, shot out all the bullets as if I was releasing my body of all the sins and guilt. I remember seeing the men digging huge holes in the ground and then feeding these giant mouths with the dead bodies of valiant warriors. It was a ritual within its own right. They covered the earth and then set fire to the mounds and mounds of dead. It all went up so easily, in one huge cloud of graying smoke. It was then so quickly ended that nothing remained as evidence to what had gone before. So simply, in one puff of smoke all of it ended and resumed as if nothing had gone before. . . .

Nicolás Durán

[In December 1915] we went to Galeana, Chihuahua, and while passing Casas Grandes we observed the switch of 25,000 Villistas over to the Constitutionalists. This newly formed alliance unleashed forty cannon discharges upon us, but we made our way safely to Galeana. The following morning we met with the Main Army of Villa. After a brief conference he decided that we should march South. We took the way from Chalchihuites, Zacatecas and it took us a full eight weeks in the rugged Sierra before we joined other bands of Villista guerrillas in Rodeo, Durango.

Many of the Villista Generals followed Señor Carranza, but Villa's favorites like Calixto Contreras, Limón Paliza, José Isabel Robles, as well as Antonio Almeida, Canuto Reyes and Benjamín Argúmedo remained loyal to him.

In the town of Rodeo we joined forces with Generals Limón, Reyes and Contreras and met the enemy in a place called Ojos Azules. Eulalio Gutierrez had been forced to resign the Presidency a short time before. Gutierrez sent troops to fight against the Villistas at the same town. When General Aguirre commanding the Zaragoza Brigade observed the Gutierrez troops, he joined their side, but when Aguirre saw that the Conventionalists were abandoning him, he joined Carranza.

When Obregon returned to the Capitol [*sic*], he received Carranza with honors. Meanwhile, we traveled to Sierra Gamon with Abraham Gonzalez' Brigade with the purpose of crossing from Torreón to Durango. In Yerba Aniz, Generals Miguel Hernandez and Canuto Reyes decided to keep only the mature soldiers and leave the younger ones. About thirty-six of us were dismissed but decided to continue the fight at our own risk. Instead of disarming we marched North. March of 1916 came and our rejected young troop continued on to Parral in search of guerrillas. We fought under General Nicolas Hernandez, our chief of operations. I finally convinced Canuto Reyes that youth was superior in battle because the young men did not run away and were not afraid of danger. We stayed for a few months with Hernandez and then joined one of the bands of Villista guerrillas that made expeditions into the Sierra into the States of Durango, Coahuila and Chihuahua.

With [Felipe] Angeles again leading us we entered the City of Chihuahua and captured 200 cannons from the Carrancistas. Under Benjamin Argumedo we tried to take the City of Torreón which was defended by General Talamantes and General Fortunato Maycotte, but we were rejected. We then returned to Jimenez to defend the City from General Francisco Murgia's attack, but we were defeated. We moved on to Horcacitas, but we lost this battle too. At the end of 1916, we went to Tepehuanes, a railroad station, we were about 1,000 men and we were attacked by surprise by the supporters of Joaquin Amaro, who had become a Carrancista. This was a bloody battle. I was hit by two bullets in the buttocks, one of which struck a bone which has forever since affected my walk and my life. I was very ill and poorly attended for two weeks.

When I remember the Revolution I find very deep within me a sacred sentiment, a sort of veneration, for the Mexican woman. I have never before expressed this feeling. I will let my heart and my memory speak the words for the women of the Revolution:

She was the soul of the Revolution because of her loyalty, her cooperation and because she dedicated all her will to suffering.

She wore light clothes, but tore them to cover the bleeding wounds, not only for her own man, but of those of his comrades.

She fought side by side with the men, bravely firing a weapon. I sadly saw thousands of dead women in the battle field.

She suffered with courageous resignation; whether it was the cold trembling of her fragile body in the mountains or the burning of flesh in the deserts.

She was constantly alert, always managing to find food even though there was always a great scarcity of it. She was always willing to share her small portion with the men.

She was huddled up at night with her man bringing warmth and sweetness to their life. If the enemy attacked by surprise, she died there after fighting by his side.

She crawled into the middle of the battle, risking her life to bring the men a hot coffee, or a bite to eat, and always an encouraging word.

She was an angel for the soldier; lighting his spirit so that he could reach victory because that meant the realization of the ideals of the Revolution and dignity for his sons and future generations.

She knew that after defeat in battle a great state of sadness, disillusionment, and depression would come over her men. When the silence hung heavy she would begin to sing. Her mouth would be dry and her stomach empty, but she sang her tune to distract and comfort the men for she knew that hunger and thirst were of little importance during these times.

She was aware of the social condition she was placed in when she followed the troops into battle. Many men were forced to become soldiers. The times were extremely trying ones, but she wanted to be close to the men and share the hardships with them.

She received her newborn child in the most primitive surroundings. She would wrap him, protecting his small body with her own from the cold and dust of the roads, and then she would continue to follow the men.

She was the Adelita, or Lupe, or Maria, Valentina, or Jesucita. With her gentle ways she would never say "my man" but rather "our men."

Once General Villa gave me an order to inform the troops that the women would not be allowed to follow. However, I disobeyed him because I knew that without the women we were worthless.

The Federal troops also had this valuable feminine element with them. Their women were called "guachas" or "Galletas"; they were no less heroines than our own Adelitas, but were never as brave or gallant in trying to match their courage with the men. They also lacked the understanding of the ideals which we were voluntarily fighting to reach. It was this understanding and determination and sacrifice which won the admiration for our Adelitas of the North Division.

After I was wounded in Tepehuanes, we concentrated our troops in Santa Rosalia. I recuperated from my wounds and at the beginning of January we went into battle against Francisco Murgia. We lost this exchange and moved on to Parral experiencing other defeats.

In Aguascalientes I was promoted to the rank of Lieutenant.

We marched on to Rosario which was my last battle. I became very ill with typhoid and with the help of my assistant I went to El Paso, Texas, where the epidemic was being treated. I entered a hospital and from 100 other patients I was one of the lucky few to survive.

March 1917 found me outside the hospital, defeated but not conquered, my wounds badly closed, my fingers missing, many physical limitations and before me an unknown world. For a moment I felt depressed. However, the New Constitution was being endorsed and I felt with satisfaction the triumph of the Revolution.

Maria Villasana López

I was born in Chihuahua in 1902 and was only eight years old when the Revolution began. What I remember most vividly about those early days was the countless number of dead people. . . .

The North Division army began its activities in Chihuahua and Durango. General Murgia, Jacinto Trevino, and Eduardo Hernandez battled against Villa in Orcacitas in 1916 and Villa lost the battle and fled to the Sierra. Before they left the area General Bonilla kidnapped me and another officer took my younger sister from our home. My mother wept and pleaded for them to leave us with her, but not our tears, our panic, or our screams helped at all.

I was given a rifle just like the other women, but I was never brave enough to use it to kill. I did help in washing the wounds of the soldiers and in caring for the sick. Many times we were half naked from making bandages with our clothes. My sister had a baby girl at the end of 1917, and I had my daughter in February of 1918.

I fought alongside General Bonilla and stayed with him, but then he too was shot and my desperation became worse. I was expecting a child and was frightened of being abandoned in the Sierra. The snow, the hunger, and the lack of clothing; alone without the protection of my daughter's father and suffering along with the many wounded men, I could only cry for our situation. When we wanted to get warm we would get close to the horses. We could not go back to our homes for the way was dangerous and we felt that we had been discredited. Crying could not help us and with nowhere to turn I decided to immigrate to the United States.

18

MARCELO CARAVEO

Fighting without Pay

1911

General Marcelo Caraveo was another military leader from Chihuahua. He joined Madero's revolution in 1910. In this selection from his unpublished memoirs, he relates how early in the Revolution, immediately after the victory at Ciudad Juárez in 1911, it became apparent that the rewards of the rebellion were going not to those who fought bravely, but to the civilian latecomers. Caraveo's disillusionment continued through the years, as he later broke with Madero and joined Orozco, then Huerta, then Zapata, and ultimately Obregón.

The revolutionaries confronted another difficult problem: the lack of currency, food, etc. Until then, operating in the field where there were shortages, the soldiers of the Revolution received irregular pay, maintained their own uniforms and military equipment, and supplied their own livestock, getting them from wherever they could.

Offering formal receipts for all they took, they would repay with the triumph of the cause. But in the city bordering on the United States [Ciudad Juárez], whose government and people were watching closely, it was not convenient to use violence to obtain resources. The First Chief of the Revolution [Carranza] gave orders that prohibited looting or disorderly behavior with the promise of severe punishment.

And with few exceptions these orders were obeyed. But then the people asked what they were going to eat, where were they going to stay. At first these were just questions, but after some days they became demands accompanied by curses.

And these exigencies became harsher and more threatening when the soldiers saw that Sr. Madero and his entourage of civilians, many of whom were latecomers to the revolution who had not smelled the gunpowder, nor faced danger, nor known the hardships of the campaign, were passing much of their time at banquets and parties they attended.

From Marcelo Caraveo, "Memoirs," unpublished manuscript, 1931, p. 46, Special Collections, University of Texas at El Paso. Translated by Mark Wasserman.

19

ANITA BRENNER AND GEORGE LEIGHTON

Photographs of Soldiers and Soldaderas

ca. 1910–1920

When Revolution erupted in Mexico in 1910, photographers flocked there. Americans were especially drawn to the action south of the border. Some of them, like Jimmy Hare and Edward Laroque Tinker, became quite famous. The best known Mexican photographer was Agustín Victor Casasola. His enormous collection of photographs taken by himself and others alone provides us with a stunning, realistic view of the everyday life of the Revolution. The photographs presented here illustrate the participation of the Mexican masses—men, women, and children—in the wars. Included, too, is an iconic photograph of Pancho Villa charging off to battle on horseback.

Anita Brenner was a Mexican-born author and magazine editor, who as a girl experienced the Revolution up close. The Wind That Swept Mexico *is a collection of her essays on the history of the Revolution. George R. Leighton put together the 184 photographs that make up most of the book. He was also an author and wrote an introduction to the collection.*

From Anita Brenner, *The Wind That Swept Mexico: The History of the Mexican Revolution* (Austin: University of Texas Press, 1971), photographs 86, 92, 93, 103.

20

Adelita

ca. 1910–1920

A corrido *is a song that tells the story of a heroic figure or tragic event or relates an odd or funny tale. The Mexican Revolution provided much material for corrido writers. "Adelita" is the most famous corrido of the Revolution. It is a tribute to the "universal" soldadera. As with all corridos, there are many versions of the lyrics.*

If Adelita ever left with another
I would follow her by land and by sea
If by sea, in a powerful warship
If on land on a military train.

If I die in battle
and my body will be
buried in the Sierras
Adelita, I implore you
cry for me.

Women and men
Give their lives for their country
with valor
Valentina, Jesusita already fought
but they never die
Adelita never dies
always fighting by the side of her soldier.

From Elizabeth Salas, *Soldaderas in the Mexican Military: Myth and History* (Austin: University of Texas Press, 1990), 92–93.

4

Civilians' Lives

The *pacíficos*, or noncombatants, comprised the great majority of Mexicans during the Revolution. Although most were enthusiastic at first, their ardor may well have diminished when the soldiers took all their crops and livestock. Staples were scarce and very expensive. The various factions printed their own money, valid only when a particular faction controlled a certain area. The paper currency was worthless. The lack of credible currency caused prices to rise. Inflation was particularly severe between 1915 and 1917, when agricultural production plummeted, creating shortages and causing increased prices. Urban areas suffered badly because country people now consumed what they had once sold in the cities. Work was hard to find, because as the military took over the railroads, many factories and mines closed for lack of transportation.

21

GREGORIO LÓPEZ Y FUENTES

El Indio

1937

One famous novel of the Revolution, El Indio *(The Indian), presents a stark depiction of the lives of indigenous peoples in Mexico before, during, and after the Revolution. López y Fuentes was born in a small village in the state of Veracruz, so he had considerable experience among country*

From Gregorio López y Fuentes, *El Indio*, trans. Anita Brenner (New York: Bobbs-Merrill, 1937), 197–99.

people. In this excerpt, he illustrates how one Indian village fell victim to
the war. The various armies took the village's crops and its young men.
The Indians cared nothing for ideology and allied with no group. All
they wanted was to be left alone. None of the characters in the novel have
names.

Something very serious was happening among the *gente de razón*.[1] Some
of the Indians who had been working for the influential people in town
brought news one day that a band of armed men had arrived suddenly,
removed the authorities, and killed the military commander.

They, the Indians, had therefore left, especially as the new people
did not seem to need them for anything. One old man said that when
he was very young, he had been fortunate enough to witness some of
the struggles among the whites, since they also war among themselves
just as Indians do. He gave examples of family feuds, which are carried on in undying hatred, each side seeking to harm the other, even by
witchcraft, until fathers and sons and their sons are all dead. The only
difference between Indians and whites is this, said the old man: that the
whites make war more efficiently, by means of the *amochitl*, the lead
used in firearms.

Either from fear or because the officials and the hacienda owners
did not call for their customary services, the Indians did no more work
in the haciendas, much less go to their weekly shifts in town. Several
months went by like this. Then the thunder of guns was heard for one
whole night, and after that came an order to contribute fodder and tortillas because a large detachment of cavalry had entered the town.

So the Indians went down the road, one behind the other, like ants
laying up provisions at the approach of the rainy season: some with a
bundle of hay on their shoulders, others carrying baskets piled high
with tortillas. The supplies were a tax levied on the rancheria [village]
and had been equally distributed among the inhabitants.

This went on for several weeks. The Indians were indifferent to what
the struggling bands called themselves. They were guided by personal
liking for some of the leaders, or merely by fear of the consequences if
they disregarded orders.

One night they heard heavy firing again. It died down at dawn, but
after daybreak the rattling went on without interruption for several

[1] *gente de razón*: People of reason. This was the name given to the middle class, or
white people in general, implying the inferiority of indigenous peoples.

hours. The defenders of the site were forced to retreat: so it was said by those who were by the road, and saw them pass hurriedly, in a sweat, stamped with the unmistakable air of people in flight. And thus passed, as the years went by, big detachments and little ones. . . .

A long time afterward one of the leaders climbed up to the village and broke the now customary calm of the heights, which the Indians had come to believe would last forever. What happened was that the head of a troop, not knowing the region, had lost himself during the hurried march. He demanded provisions, and also drafted a levy of twenty young men to serve him as "guides"; but he gave them rifles at once, and made them take the van. They never came back.

22

GUILLERMO BONFIL BATALLA

My Village during the Revolution

1984

In 1984, the Mexican scholar Guillermo Bonfil Batalla, under the auspices of the Museo Nacional de Culturas Populares (National Museum of Popular Cultures), embarked on a project to record the memories of people who had lived through the Revolution as children or young adults. The goal was to capture not the grand events, but the little happenings of survival. Mexico City especially suffered during the ongoing wars. Its residents were hard-pressed to procure even the basic necessities of life, including food. In the first account here, Manuel Servín Massieu describes how the people of Mexico City became desperate and at times acted violently. In the second account, Antonio Ortiz Casas remembers that the villages in the countryside endured many of the same shortages, having been robbed of their staples by marauding armies, who paid for their plunder with worthless money. In the final story, Nefi Fernández Acosta and María Clementina Estabean Martínez recount the dangers of the countryside. Because there were no uniformed armies, it was

From *Mi pueblo durante la Revolución* (Mexico City: Instituto Nacional de Antropología e Historia, 1985), 1:45–47, 2:71–73. Translated by Mark Wasserman.

impossible to differentiate between soldiers and civilians. When one of the warring groups found someone they did not know traveling along a road, they showed no mercy. Undoubtedly, many unaffiliated civilians were tortured or killed as a result.

Manuel Servín Massieu, Mexico City, son of Bernardo and Aurelia (born 1903 or 1904)

I remember that one of the aspects of the Revolution that impressed my mother, a girl who lived on the outskirts of Mexico City, was the concept of change and of the extreme violence that appeared and disappeared suddenly without prior warning.

Hunger frequently was linked to these changes. It was traumatic for her to see two brothers die from starvation after having lived a life, if not comfortable, then with the bare necessities. The family had had income before the Revolution, because her father had been a soldier. When he received his discharge from the army, he was left without income. The family's finances were ruined, and he had no way of earning an income. My mother felt very anxious. She looked at everything to cut expenses. She had less to eat and more to take care of. Every day she observed this pain, and she came to a decision. She would leave the house each day during certain hours, supposedly walking in the neighborhood. Instead she gathered wild greens.

One afternoon, returning with her haversack laden with greens, hunger and death crossed her road. She saw a crowd of one hundred to two hundred people protesting vigorously on the corner in front of the entrance to a yellow house with a large wooden door. They shouted Eat! Eat! Wheat! Corn! Food!! Down with the Spaniards! My mother told me that she could not get close for fear of the mob. The events happened rapidly before her eyes. Someone had informed on the Spaniards who lived in the house, accusing them of being hoarders. They were suspected of having sacks of wheat, corn, beans, and sugar. The Spaniards' store was closed, but the family's children seemed fatter than ever. How was this possible when the other people of the barrio were haggard and sad? She remembered that some adults had begun to comment that this house had no children who looked for food, nor adults who trapped cats. What were they eating? everyone asked. My mother said that there was much mistrust among the neighbors. The mob threw rocks and entered the house. The mob sacked the house violently. There were four or five dead bodies.

Antonio Ortiz Casas, Santa Cruz Amilpas, Oaxaca (born 1910)

First the Constitutionalists arrived with their almost yellow uniforms, in search of wheat, and they unfortunately found it, put it in sacks, then took it away, paying in shining paper money (*bilimbiques*) that no one would accept, not even the same government.

Then came the crude, hated Zapatistas in search of corn, and they unfortunately found it, then carried it away, and also paid with *bilimbiques* that were worthless.

Then the train brought young women from the city in search of food. Slyly they sold little articles of haberdashery at cheap prices for roosters, eggs, and grains like garbanzos, beans, and lentils.

My father, who was no longer the local political boss of [the village of] Ocotlán contracted with a guard named Adrián and gave him a 30-30 rifle and ammunition. Adrián was supposed to travel through the lands cultivated in corn, because when the first green shoots appeared on the stalks people robbed the corncobs.

Nefi Fernández Acosta and María Clementina Estabean Martínez, Tampamolón, San Luis Potosí

In these days of war there was much anxiety among the people. No one could leave their home or their village without running the risk of falling into the hands of the revolutionaries. The roads were watched by both factions according to their respective territories, and those who had the misfortune to be surprised on the roads were whipped and hung upside down in order to force them to admit to which side they belonged. And in the cases where they were enemies or simply could not explain their origins because of their fear or the torture they had endured, they were killed by hanging.

23

EDITH HENRY

The Death of Frank Henry
1916

Thousands of foreigners went to Mexico before and after the Revolution to work in the country's mines. Frank Henry accepted a position as an assayer for a British company in Guanajuato in 1905. He brought with him his wife, Edith, and their child, Ronald. They subsequently had two more children, Jessie and Kathleen. Frank held a succession of positions in various mining operations through 1914, when he moved his family to Mexico City to keep them safe. After the defeat of Victoriano Huerta later that year, Henry found a job as the superintendent in a mine near the town of San Miguel, in Zacualpan, on the border between the states of México and Guerrero. Unfortunately, the town became the site of bitter fighting between the Zapatistas and the Carrancistas. A band of Zapatistas killed Henry during a raid on his home in early 1916. The events leading to his death are described in a letter from Edith Henry to her brother a few months later, after she had returned to England following a harrowing escape from Mexico.

For about six weeks before Christmas of 1915 we had a very anxious time. Frank was much troubled, and we considered the ways and means of getting out. But it seemed impossible to get through so long a distance without animals to carry us. The Zapatistas had taken them all.

At last, a few days before Xmas, our Camp was relieved by the Carrancistas and the Zaps fled. The Carrancistas brought in such good news of the success of their army that we thought peace was at last come. They told us our part was the last bit of Mexico to be put in order. We did not need to leave after all. We had only them to believe, as there was no other way of getting news. The Carrancistas made joyful festivity with several dances and a large picnic.

All went well until the night of January 2nd. On January 1st Frank even took us out for a picnic to a nearby river and we had a glorious

---

From Edith Henry to her brother, spring 1916. Collection of Julia Swanson.

time. I brought out all the things I had hidden away—our most precious possessions. Everything was prosperous in Zacualpan, and with us.

It was 10 o'clock on Sunday evening, January 2nd. Suddenly, in rushed the Spaniard who lived nearby. Breathlessly, he told us, "The Carrancistas are going and are even now saddling up." We considered what to do. The night was pitch dark and not a mule or donkey was to be had. In one hour they had all gone, and many people as well. Frank decided: "We will stay and brave it out as we have done before, but," he said, "I would give 10 years of my life if only you and the children were in safety."

The morning of January 3rd Frank got up long before breakfast and was out and about to see how things lay. There seemed nothing alarming, so we decided to make no move (we could have abandoned our things and house and taken to the hills). It was quiet, and though we felt uneasy, there were no signs of any Zapatistas near. However, at 1 o'clock, just as we were having lunch, a small band of them came into town, and soon we heard that looting had started in some houses.

Around 2:30 in the afternoon a band of six men came and demanded we open our door. Frank showed them the "salvo conducto" paper we had received from General Molino a month previously, stating we were not to be molested. They read it and went away apparently satisfied and we thought the danger was over.

After lunch we sat out on the verandah, Frank having a cigarette, I sewing and the children playing. Somehow, we got anxious even though no one came to tell us that more men were entering the town from all parts until at last they were at least 150 all told. Mr. Odgers, the old Cornishman who lived nearby came rushing in saying that the bandits were at his house taking everything he had. He was almost beside himself. We comforted him all we could, and indeed were so busy with his troubles that we forgot our own nearly. We had a tiny amount of brandy I had saved, so I brought it—and Frank made Mr. Odgers drink it all. But I could not help see a wistful look pass over Frank's face as he did it, as if he would have given anything for a drink himself, but it was all we had.

Well, we were terribly worried, the guns had been brought out and examined that they were all right and put back into their hiding places.

. . . Feeling somewhat better, Mr. Odgers went off to deal with what was left in his house. . . .

. . . I thought a cup of tea would do us all good, so I went out to the kitchen to see if the kettle was boiling. As I passed I looked up the hill and I saw there were men galloping down towards our house. I cried out to Frank, and an instant later in rushed Ronald: "Dada, they are outside tearing down our fence and starting to climb over." Without a word to either of us, his face white and set, Frank rushed to get his gun. Ronald said: "I will go with you, Dada." I cried out to him: "No, come in with me," and Frank went out without a word to either of us, in a tremendous hurry, with the hand holding the gun behind his back so that it should not be seen until he had had time to speak with the bandits. I prepared to do my work just as we had always arranged together if it should happen. "Don't speak to me as I shall be in too great a hurry to attend to you, but just gather the children together in the bedroom and stay quietly there until you hear further from me." I did so and left the door ajar for easy access for Frank. That was the last time I saw Frank alive.

Then the shots rang out, a tremendous number of them, and the noise was terrific—of horses galloping down, running away, and hideous shouts from the bandits. The children screamed. The servant ran in—then I heard heavy footsteps on the balcony, and in rushed two men—bandits, who seized me by the arms. They yelled: "Where is your money?" and oh, so many words, cursing and furious they were—they pushed me: "Get out your things." I got out my keys, my hands shook too much to open more than one drawer, but my jewelry and money were there. They grabbed and pushed over these, and were so busy that I, unnoticed, ran out with the children. As we rushed onto the veranda—by this time the house was full of these men, and oh, I cannot tell you much more of what happened. They tore off my wedding ring—we were prisoners—a dozen guns were pointed at me—I tried to get out but was not allowed. I came back into one of the rooms—"Where is your husband?" they kept saying. I felt better. Frank must be alive yet I thought, but he must be wounded and someone has hidden him. They were all more or less drunk. They called us Americans—I said: "We are not, we're English, that's our flag," and pointed at the Union Jack on our wall. "All the same," they replied.

They demanded money and our weapons, and with the muzzle of a gun at my head I showed where the other two guns were, and where my silver teapot and a few other things were hidden. All this time Kathleen was screaming and trembling with fright. "If you have no pity for us, at any rate have pity on this poor little girl—have you no heart at all," I asked them. They replied: "We want money." "I have none—you have taken it all," had no effect on them. Plunder was all that was on their minds. Their beastly faces were shoved into mine, jeeringly—"Where is your husband?" General Molino, who had given us our salvo conducto, was with them, and he said: "How much will you pay me if I let you go?" I replied: "The men have already taken all I have."

After I repeated this many times they seemed convinced it was true, and at last we were allowed to escape. As we rushed across the yard, a man tried to stop us—he lifted his gun to strike Ronald with the butt end. I saw it falling and pulled Ronald with all my might, and the man with the force of the blow fell over forward, but the gun had just caught Ronald's arm.

We ran on to the gate to get out, and there I saw Frank just outside in the road stretched out. One glance showed me he was dead. He had been shot from behind right through the heart. Evidently he was just turning to slip back into the house when one man who had hidden himself in the house opposite, calmly waited for Frank to turn his back and then taken aim.

As I saw Frank I rushed forward and knelt down beside him. Many horses and a few men were there. One man leveled his gun at me, with his finger ready to shoot—"Touch him and we shoot"—I raised Frank's hand to my lips, it was already cold and stiff. Then taking the children I rushed away to hide. I could do nothing for Frank now, and there were the children to save.

We wandered about dazed for a while. The town was like a dead town—not a soul to be seen, except the men carrying loot out of our house, and the noise of breaking up of other houses. Up the hill I saw our servant Leopoldo beckoning silently to us. We sat there in his house in the dark—Ronald hugging his injured arm, without one tear in his eyes, just silently without a word until nightfall. Then we stayed there for the night as we could not go to the house.

24

FRANK GALVÁN

Escaping the Revolution

1973

Many Mexicans fled from the destruction and dangers of the Revolution, including those who had worked for or allied with the Díaz regime. In 1973, Mary Lee Nolan of Texas A&M University interviewed a number of these exiles, including Frank Galván. Galván's father, a federal government bureaucrat, was forced to flee Mexico in 1913, when Huerta overthrew Madero. Temporarily, he left his family behind, and they struggled to make ends meet. He soon returned for them, however, and led them on an adventurous trip across the border. As this excerpt shows, people from all classes and from every faction endured hardships during the Revolution.

FG: My name is Frank J. Galvan, Jr. I was born in Santa Barbara, Chihuahua, Mexico on February 11, 1908, and I am 65 years of age.

ML [Mary Lee Nolan]: When did you leave Mexico?

FG: We left Mexico sometime in middle of 1913. We left Mexico from our point of origin which was Santa Barbara, Chihuahua, Mexico. Our father had been a federal government employee in the city of Santa Barbara and at the outbreak of the Revolution he was branded as a Cientifico. Things got a little dangerous for him so he fled from Santa Barbara to [the city of] Chihuahua incognito and from Chihuahua, it is believed that he left as far from Mexico as possible. I am under the impression that he finally reached his destination somewhere in Canada.

ML: Did you and your family go with him then?

FG: No. He left the family all in the town of Santa Barbara, Chihuahua. We had a home; a two story home, and while he was away—it looked

From Frank Galván, interview by Mary Lee Nolan, March 14, 1973, Mexican Revolution Project, Oral History Collections, Cushing Library, Texas A&M University, College Station.

to me like it was years—we were penniless, poverty-stricken and had to exist by converting the upper story of the house into a rooming house. There was a yard in the center of the house and a second yard to the rear that used to be called two patios, one for the servants and the other for the members of the household.

Anyway we managed to exist during the Revolution by selling *yerba buena*. There was a farm nearby and we used to go pick up the peppermint, get it into bunches, and sell it on the street. That continued for a considerable, to me, length of time and the source of our income we had then was from the sale of this *yerba buena* and the rental of the upper story of this house.

ML: How many were there in your family?

FG: There were living with us, my mother, Oscar, Raymond, Frank, Henry, and Josephine. . . .

Anyway, one night there was a strange knock at the door and here was father. He had returned to Santa Barbara incognito, disguised as a proletariat, or revolutionary peasant, with a great big sombrero. Shortly thereafter, maybe immediately, we were placed in a mule-drawn wagon with all our personal belongings that we could hurriedly obtain. We left early in the morning even before dawn for El Valle [de] Allende, a close town. I didn't know our destination but I knew we were leaving Santa Barbara in a hurry. We stayed in El Valle, probably for a couple of days, obtaining the necessary provisions for our trip. Then we took off through the back roads of Mexico and then I realized that we were fleeing from the Mexican Revolution and that we were going to a territory or a place under the control of the Federal troops. . . .

. . . We journeyed, I think, to Conchos. In Conchos we got sheltered in an old abandoned grocery store. There was a man in the grocery store lying in bed with about eight or ten stab wounds in his upper breast or chest. We heard the story with great admiration and fright about his being assaulted the night before by a gang of rebels. We remained in this Conchos, I think that was the name of the city, and then we took off to a crossing of the Rio Conchos. It was the most exciting manner in which we crossed the river. The river was very high and the mules were pulling and trying to get the wagon across the channel and the floor of the entire wagon was inundated. We just didn't want it to meet with disaster and we pulled it across the Rio Conchos. Later, if I remember, the next experience of any great importance was arriving at the military camp, Point Nica. Much to our surprise the military command was under the command of a fellow by the name of Chao. The reason I remember the name is that Mother told us that Mr. Chao had been a friend of the Mata family. There they apprehended my father and put him under a personal recognizance arrest. He remained with us, but we all knew that my father had been arrested by the Revolutionary forces and one early morning. . . .

. . . I don't know what happened, but my father was able to leave that Mexican revolutionary encampment and got on the road and left for the city of Chihuahua.

ML: Were you still with him at the time—the whole family?

FG: The whole family. So we came to Chihuahua. Nearing the road of Chihuahua, father decided to put up a white flag and beat the thunder out of the mules and raced to the fortification of the military lines of the federal troops. It was after we had been machine-gunned and shot at and had lost a mule. Anyway we got into the protection of the federal forces who permitted us to get into the city. They escorted us and told us which way to go to the city-proper of Chihuahua. We remained in the city for about 10 days while the city was besieged by the Mexican Revolutionary forces. . . .

. . . And we picked up sister Helen who was attending the Palmore College. About a week later there was a special train, a military train with three coaches for passengers. That train left Chihuahua and we were on that train headed for Juarez. The trip from Chihuahua City to Juarez took approximately 15 days. This train was made up of boxcars, probably 20 or 30 boxcars. Each boxcar was loaded with Mexican federal troops and they had some platforms on which they had artillery pieces and at the rear of the train there were three cars, full of refugees—a lot of Americans coming from Mexico to Juarez. The trip was very eventful. There was a lot of fighting; skirmishes between the federal government troops and Mexican Revolutionary forces. We had to stop sometimes two or three times a day to ward off the rebels. And nearly every time that the train stopped to engage the Revolutionary forces in combat we would lose two or three freight cars that had to be thrown off the tracks, off onto the side of the rail. Then we hitched the remaining cars together and pulled off. I remember on numerous occasions that the bridges had been burnt and we had to take railroad ties from the places immediately that we had just passed, and use those railroad ties in building bridges across the railroad bridges that had been destroyed by the Revolutionary forces. . . .

... We just kept going forward to Juarez. And when we got here in Juarez there was a battle going on. The engine and the three passenger cars were the only thing that was able to reach Juarez. As I've stated before, the trip took us about 15 days. Of course during that time our provisions and the food supplies had been exhausted. We were hungry and tired. We left the railroad train at 16th of September street and the railroad crossing in Juarez. We ran all the way from there to the Santa Fe Bridge ... until we got to the American Santa Fe immigration station.

5

Revolutionary Politics

The various revolutionary factions squabbled endlessly. There was also a continuous counterrevolution. As we have seen, the Madero Revolution fractured almost immediately, with Zapata and Orozco leading opposition in the south and north, respectively. The revolutionaries then coalesced once again in opposition to Huerta and his reactionary regime. After the original Constitutionalists, the successors to the Maderistas, defeated Huerta, they split into Constitutionalists, led by Carranza, and Conventionalists, led by Villa and Zapata (who had united around a convention in Aguascalientes in 1914). Carranza won out in the end, but the maneuvering and scheming among the Constitutionalists was as legendary as their propensity for corruption. Simultaneously, the remaining conservative opposition to the Revolution continued its adamant resistance.

25

MARTÍN LUIS GUZMÁN

The Eagle and the Serpent

1928

The novel The Eagle and the Serpent, *originally published in 1928, presents a cynical view of the maneuvering within the Constitutionalist ranks to enrich and empower their leaders. It is a very disheartening portrayal of the revolutionary intelligentsia and bureaucracy.*

From Martín Luis Guzmán, *The Eagle and the Serpent*, trans. Harriet de Onís (Garden City, N.Y.: Dolphin Books, 1965), 55–57, 111, 149, 229, 236.

One time we were sitting around the table after dinner, as usual, fifteen or twenty of us. . . . We were all feeling good. That morning the military band had marched through the town twice playing reveille to celebrate the two latest victories of our troops, at Chihuahua and Tepic. With this motive, Carranza began to pontificate, as usual, and finally set up, as an indisputable fact, the superiority of an improvised and enthusiastic army over a scientifically organized one. A statement of this sort must perforce smack of heresy to any trained soldier, and it did so that night. [Felipe] Angeles waited until Carranza had finished and then, gently in the phrasing, but most energetically in his arguments, rose to the defense of the art of warfare as something that can be learned and taught and that can be better exercised the better one has studied it. But Carranza, despotic in his conversations as in everything else, interrupted his Minister of War brusquely with this bald statement, closing the matter:

"In life, General," he said, "especially in leading and governing men, the only thing that is necessary or useful is goodwill."

Angeles took a sip from his coffee cup and did not utter another syllable. All the rest of us kept quiet, and the final words of the First Chief floated in the silence that hung over us. "Is it going to end like this?" I wondered. "It isn't possible. Somebody will surely put things in their proper place."

But, unfortunately, more than a minute elapsed before anyone made a move to speak. Don Venustiano savored in silence the pleasure of dictating over even our ideas. Perhaps he enjoyed the spectacle of our servility and cowardice. I do not know whether I did right or not. A feeling of shame overwhelmed me. I remembered that I had thrown in my lot with the Revolution, and that to do this I had been obliged to sacrifice all my previous life; I felt myself on the horns of a dilemma. Either my rebellion against Victoriano Huerta was senseless or I was duty-bound to protest here, too, even if only by word.

The silence about the table continued even more dense than before. Was that going to stop me? Decidedly not. I flung myself head first into the small adventure that would immediately classify me forever among the dissenters and malcontents of the revolutionary field.

"Isn't it queer?" I said, without hedging, looking straight into the depths of the First Chief's benignant eyes; "I think just the opposite. I absolutely reject the theory that goodwill can replace ability and efficiency. The saying, 'Hell is paved with good intentions' seems to me a very wise one, because those whose chief characteristic is goodwill are always taking on tasks that are beyond their strength, and that is their weakness. It may be because I haven't been out of school long, but I am an ardent believer in books and training and I detest improvisations and makeshifts, except when they cannot be avoided. I believe that from a political standpoint technique is a vital necessity for Mexico, at least in three fundamental aspects, finance, public education, and war."

My outburst produced stupefaction rather than surprise. Don Venustiano looked at me with a benevolent air, so benevolent that I at once understood that he would never forgive my audacity. With the exception of [Rafael] Zubarán, who flashed me a glance of friendly understanding, Angeles, who looked at me approvingly, and [Alberto] Pani, who showed his solidarity with me in enigmatic smiles, nobody raised his eyes from the tablecloth. And only Adolfo de la Huerta, trying to turn the whole thing off as a kind of joke, came to my support, or rather to my assistance. He did everything he could to efface the bad impression my presumptuousness had left on Carranza's mind. This was a brave and honorable act on his part, born of his conciliatory spirit, for he did it at the risk of falling into disfavor himself. . . .

General Iturbe offered me, through Colonel Eduardo Hay, a military post in his brigade which held out not a few attractions. I was to be lieutenant-colonel and assistant chief of staff. . . . I could not bring myself to trade my precious independence of word and action for the stiff discipline of the soldier, and one of the reasons for not doing so was that I saw no reason for making such a sacrifice. I had no political or military ambitions; and, besides, the principal leaders of the Revolution were far from being, in my opinion, unselfish and idealistic enough for me to want to bind myself to them, even indirectly, with chains that are always dangerous and not always easy to break. . . .

The idea of joining the First Chief's entourage did not appeal to me in the least. Within Don Venustiano's orbit intrigue and the lowest kind of sycophancy grew rank; the trimmers, the tale-bearers, the bootlickers, the panderers had the inside track. And even though there were moments when this nauseous atmosphere was dissipated by the presence of men of a completely different caliber, . . . the honest men, those who were ready to stand up and be counted for their principles, were wasting their time in that completely partisan circle, unless they had such important duties that they could not be abandoned. It was idle to conceive false hopes. By this time I had learned a lot and knew that Carranza, old and stubborn, would never change. He would go on responding to flattery rather than acts, to servility rather than ability. To the day of his death he would be influenced by abjectness, pettiness, for he himself, whose make-up was totally devoid of greatness, was not free from essential paltriness. His calculating coldness, which the incense bearers called the gift of a great statesman, was useful to him in measuring the picayune, not the great, with the result that he ruined his finest moments. Who ever saw in him any display of real enthusiasm, official or private, toward the great events of the Revolution? He was not magnanimous even in rewarding. . . .

"Carranza," I said, "is nothing but a self-seeking politician who is devilishly shrewd at turning to his own advantage his training in the old school of Mexican politics. There is no real sense of civic duty or ideals of any kind in the man. Nobody who is not a flatterer and bootlicker, or that doesn't pretend to be to further his personal ambitions with Carranza's help, can work with him. He systematically corrupts people; he fans the evil passions, the petty intrigues, even dishonesty, in those who surround him, so he can better manage and hold the whip hand over them. There is not a revolutionist with any personality, or even sincerely devoted to the cause, who, unless he has been willing to let himself be used as a tool, has not been obliged to break with him or accept an insignificant, humiliating role. And those who have not yet openly broken with him are on tenterhooks and don't know what attitude to take. You know as well as I do that many of our friends are in one of these two situations. This is what has happened or is happening with Maytorena, with Angeles, with Villarreal, with Blanco, with Vasconcelos, with Bonilla, and even with you. You remember the rebuffs and secret hostility with which he treated you when we were in Nogales. The truth is that Carranza dreams of the possibility of becoming another Porfirio Díaz, a bigger and better Porfirio Díaz, for at heart he admires and venerates his memory. Isn't it apparent that Carranza is trying to turn everything to this one end, and that he doesn't care a rap about the good the Revolution might bring to Mexico? You know perfectly well that from the first moment Carranza has systematically kept the Revolution divided against itself. . . ."

. . . The explanation of what took place while Carranza was in power is to be found, better than in anything else, in the voluntary confusion that sprang up between *meum* and *tuum*, the confusion having to do with taking, not giving. Without this peculiarly characteristic detail his rule becomes an almost unintelligible political phenomenon. One cannot otherwise understand the historical significance—as apart from the merely individual—of the private acts of many of Carranza's close followers, nor the culminating moments in the political events of these days and shortly afterward: the official looting of the banks, the paper-money scandal in Veracruz, and the standardization of the currency.

It is curious how the public, so prone to make mistakes—notwithstanding what is said to the contrary—and so inclined to attribute heroism and grandeur to clay-footed gods, hit the nail on the head in this case from the very first. From Carranza the popular fancy coined *carrancear*, and "to carranzaize" and "to steal" became synonymous. Stealing became a categorical imperative among the adherents of Carranza, in part because it was a safe, quick way of getting what they wanted, and in part a sport and amusement.

26

VENUSTIANO CARRANZA

The Agrarian Law

January 6, 1915

Venustiano Carranza was a member of a landowning family in Coahuila, in northern Mexico, who rebelled against the conservative reaction that overthrew Madero in 1913. Carranza led the Constitutionalist faction that won the Revolution. The Agrarian Law helped to convince many people in the countryside to support his cause in the civil war against Villa and Zapata. He had no intention of implementing the decree, however, and once he had won the war, he restored the land to the hacienda owners whose property had been confiscated by the revolutionary generals. Nonetheless, the decree served as the basis for much of the land reform that occurred after 1920, for others used it as a legal precedent.

The Law that Declares null all the expropriations of land, water and mountains owned by the pueblos, authorized in contravention to the Law of 25 June 1856.

VERACRUZ, JANUARY 6, 1915

From Venustiano Carranza, "Ley que declara nulas todas las enjenaciones de tierras, aguas y montes pertenecientes a los pueblos, otorgados en contravención a lo dispuesto en la ley de 25 de junio de 1856" in Graziella Altamirano and Guadalupe Villa, *La Revolución Mexicana: Textos de su Historia* (Mexico City: Secretaría de Educación Pública and Instituto de Investigaciones Dr. José María Luis Mora, 1985), 3:447–48, 3:450–53. Translated by Mark Wasserman.

Venustiano Carranza, First Chief of the Constitutionalist Army, in charge of the executive power of the United States of Mexico and the chief of the Revolution. . . .

Considering: That one of the most general causes of unease and discontent of the agricultural population of this country has been the despoiling of the communal property . . . conceded by the colonial government as a means to secure the existence of the indigenous class, and that on the pretext of complying with the Law of June 25, 1856, and other dispositions that ordered the breaking up and reduction of the pueblos' lands into private property left into the hands of speculators; . . .

That in the same case they encountered multitudes of other populations in different parts of the Republic . . . that had their origins in . . . the possession of more or less large holdings which they kept undivided for generations, water, land, and mountains. . . .

. . . That providing the means . . . to recover the lands of the many pueblos that were despoiled or obtaining that which is necessary for their well-being and development, we do not try to revive the ancient communities, nor create others similar, but only give the land to the rural population . . . so that it can fully develop its right to life and freedom from economic servitude. . . .

To accomplish this I have issued the following decree:

Article 1. Declare null:

  I. All the alienations of land, water, and mountains belonging to the pueblos, *rancherías*, *congregaciones*, or communities taken by the political bosses, governors of the states, or whatever local authority in contravention of the Law of 25 June 1856 and other pertinent laws and dispositions;

 II. All the concessions, compositions, or sales of land, water, and mountains by the Secretary of Development, Treasury, or any other federal authority from the first of December 1876 until the date with which these lands were invaded and occupied illegally. . . .

III. All of the surveys carried out during the period of time noted above by companies, judges, or other authorities of the state or federal government through which the communities were invaded illegally. . . .

Article 2. The division or distribution of the lands which are legitimately the property of these communities . . . and wrongful acts can be nullified only when two-thirds of the residents petition. . . .

Article 3. Those pueblos that because of the lack of documentation cannot succeed in restitution can obtain sufficient land to reconstitute through government expropriation of neighboring land.

Article 4. In order to put into effect this law and other agrarian laws in accordance with the political program of the Revolution, we create

1. A National Agrarian Commission of nine members, presided over by the Secretary of Development that will supervise the laws;

2. A Local Agrarian Commission, comprised of five people, for each state or territory of the Republic, with the attributes that the laws determine;

3. Executive Committees in each state with three members with the attributes to be determined.

Article 5. The executive committee will depend in each state on the Local Agrarian Commissions, while in turn [are] subordinate to the National Agrarian Commission.

Article 6. The solicitations for restitution of the lands belonging to the pueblos that were invaded and occupied illegally, and which fall under Article 1 of this law, will be presented directly to the Governors of the states in front of the highest authorities, but in cases where there is a lack of communications or a state of war makes local government action difficult, the solicitations will be also presented to the military chiefs that will be specially authorized by the Executive Power.

27

CASA DEL OBRERO MUNDIAL

The Pact with Carranza and the Establishment of the Red Battalions

1915

By 1915, the Casa del Obrero Mundial was the leading union federation in Mexico. Carranza expended considerable effort to woo urban workers to his side in the incipient civil war against Villa and Zapata, both of whom had earned widespread support in the countryside. Carranza gave the federation semiofficial status, allowed it to organize, and sided with it against foreign employers. He also funneled funds to the group. Eventually, Carranza and Obregón signed a pact with the organization, which resulted in the establishment of the Red Battalions. The six thousand union workers belonging to these battalions helped tip the balance in Carranza's favor in the crucial battles against Villa and Zapata that took place in 1915.

In view of the fact that the workers of the House of the Worker of the World adhere to the constitutionalist government headed by Citizen Venustiano Carranza, it has been agreed to put on record the relations of said government with the workers, and those of the latter with the former, in order to determine the form in which they are to give their collaboration with the constitutional cause, the following sign the present document for the purpose: . . . .

First. The constitutionalist government reiterates its resolution, stated in the decree of December 4 of the year last passed, to improve, by appropriate laws, the condition of laborers, issuing during the struggle all the laws that may be necessary to carry out that resolution.

Second. The workers of the House of the Workers of the World, for the purpose of hastening the triumph of the constitutionalist revolution and intensifying as far as possible the unnecessary shedding of blood,

From "Compact Entered into between the Constitutionalist Revolution and the House of the Worker of the World," in United States Senate, Committee on Foreign Relations, *Investigation of Mexican Affairs* (Washington, D.C.: Government Printing Office, 1920), 2:2823–24.

put on record the resolution they have taken to collaborate in an effective and practical manner for the triumph of the revolution and to take up arms either to garrison towns that are in the possession of the constitutionalist government or to fight the reaction.

Third. To carry out the provisions contained in the two preceding clauses, the constitutionalist government will, with the solicitude it has heretofore employed, attend to the just claims of the workers in the conflicts that may arise between them and their employers as a consequence of work. . . .

Fifth. The workers of the House of the Workers of the World shall make lists in each one of the towns where they are organized, and at once in the City of Mexico, including the names of all their companions who solemnly offer to comply with the provisions of clause second. The lists shall be sent as soon as they are completed to the first chief of the constitutionalist army, that he may be informed of the number of workers who are disposed to take up arms.

Sixth. The workers of the House of the Workers of the World shall make active propaganda to win the sympathy of all the workers in the Republic and of the Workers of the World for the constitutionalist revolution by demonstrating to all Mexican laborers the advantages of joining the revolution, since the latter will make effective for the laboring classes the improvements the latter seek through their groups.

Seventh. The workers shall establish revolutionary centers or committees in all the places they judge convenient to do so. The committees, besides the propaganda work, shall supervise the organization of labor groups and their collaboration in favor of the constitutionalist cause.

Eighth. The constitutionalist government shall, in case it be necessary, establish colonies of workers in zones which it has dominated to serve as a refuge for the families of the workers who have declared their adhesion to the constitutionalist cause.

Ninth. The workers who take up arms in the constitutionalist army and the workwomen who give their services for attention to and treatment of the wounded, or other similar services, shall have but one denomination whether they be organized in companies, battalions, regiments, brigades, or divisions. All shall be designated as "reds."

Constitution and reforms.

Greeting and social revolution.

Honorable Veracruz, February 17, 1915.

Signed: Rafael Zubaran, Capmany, Rafael Quintaro, Carlos M. Rincon, Rosendo Salazar, Juna Tudo, Salvador Gonzalo Garcia, Rodolfo Aguirre, Roberto Valdes, Celestino Gasca.

28

EDUARDO ITURBIDE

A Counterrevolutionary Governs the Federal District

1914

*Eduardo Iturbide was a wealthy landowner from Michoacán. President
Huerta appointed him governor of the Federal District, which included
Mexico City. The Villistas and Zapatistas despised Iturbide because he
had allegedly mistreated or killed a large number of peasants. Once the
Huerta regime crumbled, Iturbide feared for his life and arranged his
escape from the country. In this excerpt, he recounts the corruption he
faced and tries to portray himself in the best light possible. The selection
gives us a glimpse of the Revolution from the reactionary, or counterrevo-
lutionary, side.*

"I then continued working without paying any attention to politics, until
one night in January, 1914, about 2 a.m., when an aide of General Huerta
came to my house and awoke me, saying that General Huerta wished to
see me in a hurry. I dressed quickly, fearing that Huerta was about to
have me shot. I was taken to Huerta's private residence and he told me
that he knew I was courageous and energetic, for he knew I had repeat-
edly defended my ranches against the attacks of large bands of bandits.
For this reason he was going to name me Brigadier General and Governor of the Federal District. I assured him I could not accept the honours
he wished to bestow upon me, for I had five estates to attend to and they
required all my attention. . . .

"I was not molested again until . . . March, 1914. . . .

"General Huerta then repeated his proposition of January, but put
it in the form of an order, saying that he was going to levy me into the
service. I begged him to leave out the military rank and merely appoint
me as Governor. He refused, telling me that if in twenty-four hours I
was not dressed in the uniform of a Brigadier General, he would have

---

From Randolph Wellford Smith, "Governing the Federal District: Eduardo N. Iturbide's
Story," in *Benighted Mexico* (New York: John Lane, 1916), 130–33, 139–40.

me arrested and would send me to Santiago (the military prison). . . . I then told General Huerta that if he made me Governor I would insist on conducting the office in a straightforward and honourable manner. He answered that was exactly what he wanted.

"I assumed the office, and the first trouble I had was with some of Huerta's relatives and intimates, who seemed to wish to rob the State of everything it possessed. I assumed office on March 28th, taking it over from Governor Ramon Corona. I at once discovered that four of the largest gambling houses in the city had been paying graft at the rate of $5,000 a month for certain privileges, which I immediately stopped. A few days after I had assumed office, two men very near to General Huerta came to my office. One of them threw a roll of papers on my desk, saying: 'You have to send those contracts to be fixed up immediately.' I answered him, saying, 'The first thing to be done here is that you observe the proper respect toward me, for if you do not do so, I will send you to Santiago.' (The one who had spoken was a Colonel.) He then came down off his high horse and told me that General Huerta had asked me, through him, to do this for him. I then told him that while I was in office all matters had to take their due legal course. He replied by asking me to consider the matter and in the meantime he would leave the papers with me.

"The following day a young lawyer named Mendez Riva came to see me and said that the Colonel was sorry he had acted as he had the day before; that he wished me to help him in his business and would state frankly that he was to receive $300,000 in pesos for the contracts, of which sum he was willing to give me one half. I rose to my feet and told Riva I was not a thief, and pointing to the door asked him to leave my presence immediately. The next day I went to see General Huerta and related the incident to him and he replied by telling me to send such callers to hell. . . .

"There was a great deal of trouble caused me on account of food staples and prices, and it was very hard to prevent merchants from taking advantage of the circumstances to raise prices. The butchers went on a strike and I had to stop them by convincing them that they should under the circumstances try to help and not make matters worse. There were many incidents of that character."

29

LUIS GARCÍA PIMENTEL

The Oligarchy's Perspective

1912

The members of the García Pimentel family were among the most important sugar planters. They were also stubborn holdouts against Zapata's forces in Morelos. In 1912, Luis García Pimentel reported from Morelos on the continuing disruptions over land reform.

Luis García Pimentel to the Secretary of Development, Coloization, and Industry

June 6, 1912

The causes of the disturbances and anarchy that reign in the state of Morelos, in my judgment, are two principles:

1. Among those who have risen in arms there are many criminals that were freed by the rebels at the beginning of the Maderista revolution. These people understand that if they put down their arms and the state is pacified, they will have to return to their prisons for the terms pending. They prefer instead the life of plunder, fires, and other abuses they are accustomed to commit.

2. Between the rebels and the totality of what has been given the name peaceful Zapatistas exists an idea of agrarian socialism, nonsensical and devoid of reason and, of necessity, justice. They are wrong because they are in general less extensive than in the rest of Mexico and for that reason there is more divided property. There is also a great number of small properties that can be seen in the documentation of the last law of revaluation of property in the state. It is necessary to return the land because

From Luis García Pimentel to the Secretary of Development, Coloization, and Industry June 6, 1912, in the Archivo General de la Nación, Ramo de Secretaría de Gobernación, Legajo Asunto Varios, Isla María, Estados, 1911–1914, Expediente, no. 298. Translated by Mark Wasserman.

events show that the residents of Morelos have had land and did not know how to conserve it and sold it to better shepherds. The hacienda owners of Morelos assert that the distribution of land as restitution is not just and the properties in the state are in the majority legal and legitimate.

This socialist idea has its origins in the predilections of the ignorant and ambitious agitators who have favored some gubernatorial candidates who have succeeded in winning this post. It took much more than propaganda to implement this idea in the Maderista revolution. The real exploiters are the shysters and agitators who obtain too many benefits for the villages, which they trick with unrealizable and absurd promises fanning the flames of race and class.

30

FRANCISCA GARCÍA ORTIZ

Speech to the Feminist Congress in Yucatán

1916

During the Revolution, women sought not only better living and working conditions for themselves and their families but also equal treatment under the law. In January 1916, Salvador Alvarado, the radical governor of Yucatán, invited women to a convention to discuss how to improve conditions for women. García represented the most conservative approach to women's progress. Her speech seems quite mild today, emphasizing the role of education in eliminating "the yoke of tradition."

Ladies of the Convention:
    What you are about to hear is not a report derived from formal experimentation nor from experience. It is simply an opinion concerning what

Francisca García Ortiz, Speech, January 13, 1916, in Alaide Foppa and Helene F. de Aguilar, "The First Feminist Congress in Mexico, 1916," *Signs* 6, no. 1 (Autumn 1979): 197–99.

I've been able to observe in my few short years of life. So I have no fixed conclusions. I beg you, in view of this, to excuse my mistakes.

What social means should be employed to emancipate women from the yoke of tradition?

I submit that young ladies of the twentieth century no longer think with nineteenth-century minds; it can be said that all of us, without exception, hold modern ideas which tend towards the improvement of our condition. In the past the yoke which stifled all the hopes of women was clearly felt; today, no. That yoke is disappearing and we can make it vanish completely, by educating *society*: it is society which cuts off horizons and aspirations. Who forms that society? Men. Well then, let us educate men. In doing that, we will have educated women, too.

In earlier times, a woman could not be self-sufficient; she was regarded unfavorably, and of this we have many examples, occurring even nowadays. I will cite one of the many. A young woman must earn her living and starts to work in an office. One of the boss's children falls in love with her and the father of the boy makes her life miserable because she is a "common working girl," a woman who has to earn her bread. There is, on the other hand, another girl: not "decent," but the daughter of well-to-do parents, who doesn't need to work. Now *she* is the father's ideal, the wife who is suitable for his son. And that poor girl, who really has fallen in love with the fellow, weeps and perhaps even curses her life. Wasn't she the same as he, a child of honest parents, although impoverished now, only differing from the man in the fact that she must work? Whose fault is it that the working woman is regarded as an outcast? Whose fault is it that woman wavers? The man's. We should educate the man, always: always! Let us pay slight attention to women's education, but a lot—a great deal—of attention to the education of men, and above all, to their enlightenment. In the last century a woman simply could not acquire culture. Why? Because they said—because they believed—that thereby she would consider herself superior to the man, or at least, his equal. Were they mistaken? No. There are women now who *are* more civilized than their husbands, and much good may it do them if they find a husband who realizes the distance between them. I think that for a marriage to be happy there has to be love, a great deal of love. And how can we love a person we see as inferior to ourselves? I could not love that way. In order to love someone, to entrust myself to him for the rest of my life, I must consider that someone superior. Today many men are afraid of the intellectual woman. Why? Because they understand that she improves herself every day; that each day her mind advances. Should men be afraid? No. Men should make sure they are not at a disadvantage. And to this a man must be more and more enlightened.

Why were wives happy in the past century? Why was there no need for divorce? Because the woman was less cultured. She was wholly a wife, a mother. Not now. We have women who forget what they are, who give up nothing for their children. Was the woman of the past a better woman? Yes. But surely today's woman could be better? Yes, indeed. But let us spare her much suffering caused by her evolution. Let us, in fact, educate men for this new life. How can we emancipate woman from the yoke of tradition? By educating man—he who rules always, and forever. Who can influence his education? The mother. She will help us. She will see to it that her sons respect women's advancement, that they look favorably on a woman's being intellectual. Households abound in which many women have been left in the shadows—women who could have been guides for new generations merely because the brothers, or the father, have opposed her education, her learning. At a certain age the little girl is removed from school. Why should she graduate? Is she going to teach? No, poor little thing. Let's take her out so she can learn other things. She had better not get a diploma. "Teachers don't get married." Why are they afraid of the woman who has broad knowledge? Because if we were to comprehend them, if we were to regard them as less educated than we, we could not love them. We would look down on them. We would not see men as superior to us, and they would be forced to see us as better than they.

It is a fact that it is hard for an educated woman to marry. So I think it is a waste for women to be constantly educated farther along. This learning is an obstacle to woman's happiness, and it is a pity that minds so beautiful, souls so noble, should not raise progeny who might bring to fulfillment (in the future) our present desires, achieving the pinnacle of civilization. In order to commence this education of man, mothers must assist us; and mothers, if not all of them at least the majority, should constitute the Feminist Convention. We idealistic young ladies alone would be of no use, although we are future mothers: the advancement and improvement for which we yearn will take a long time yet.

Let us for God's sake educate man, our moral and social support; and let us not dominate him as many women intend, and which will be the outcome if our own development proceeds apace while his falls behind.

Please God things work out this way; otherwise we would weep bitterly over the ruins of our feminine charms, which we would ourselves have trampled into the dust. Let us never forget that the woman should always be the delight of the home, the gentle comrade of man; she may indeed overcome him through her love and sweetness. But let her not dominate him with her intellect nor with her learning.

Let women be women, always; but may men become worthier and better men.

Merida, January 13, 1916

FRANCISCA GARCÍA ORTIZ

6

The Revolution's Achievements

The Constitutionalists led by Carranza—a coalition of dissident elites, members of the middle class, and various groups of country people and workers—set about to rewrite the Constitution of 1857 and to rebuild the war-torn nation. They favored minimal changes to the constitution, mostly to ensure access to politics and government, and had no intention of implementing profound reforms. Nonetheless, with Villa and Zapata still in the field, and a radical group within the Constitutionalists led by Obregón pushing for far-reaching concessions to workers and small farmers, the constitutional convention swerved to the left and ultimately produced the most radical document of its kind up to that time. The Constitution of 1917 notwithstanding, laws were enforced on the state and local levels, and there was considerable corruption and arbitrariness even in the process of reform.

31

CONSTITUTIONAL CONVENTION

The Constitution of 1917: Article 27

1917

Article 27 included the most far-reaching reforms of the Revolution. It touched on landownership, the Roman Catholic Church, and the rights of foreigners, all of which had been the subjects of unresolved debates during the nineteenth century. Most important, the article established that

From "Political Constitution of the United States of Mexico: Article 27" in United States Senate, Committee on Foreign Relations, *Investigation of Mexican Affairs* (Washington, D.C.: Government Printing Office, 1920), 2:3126–29.

landownership was originally vested in the nation and that the nation
could expropriate land for the public good.

ART. 27. The ownership of lands and waters within the limits of the
national territory is vested originally in the nation, which has had and
has the right to transmit title thereof to private persons, thereby consti-
tuting private property.

Private property shall not be expropriated except for cause of public
utility and by means of indemnification.

The nation shall have at all times the right to impose on private property such limitations as the public interest may demand as well as the
right to regulate the development of natural resources, which are sus-
ceptible of appropriation, in order to conserve them and equitably to
distribute the public wealth. For this purpose necessary measures shall
be taken to divide large landed estates; to develop small landed holdings; to establish new centers of rural population with such lands and
waters as may be indispensable to them; to encourage agriculture and
to prevent the destruction of natural resources and to protect property
from damage detrimental to society. Settlements, hamlets situated on
private property, and communes which lack lands or water or do not
possess them in sufficient quantities for their needs shall have the right
to be provided with them from the adjoining properties, always having
due regard for small landed holdings. Wherefore, all grants of lands
made up to the present time under the [agrarian] decree of January 6,
1915, are confirmed. Private property acquired for the said purposes
shall be considered as taken for public use. In the nation is vested direct
ownership of all minerals or substances which in veins, masses, or beds
constitute deposits whose nature is different from the components of
the land, such as minerals from which metals and metaloids used for
industrial purposes are extracted; beds of precious stones, rock salt, and
salt lakes formed directly by marine waters, products derived from the
decomposition of rocks, when their exploitation requires underground
work; phosphates which may be used for fertilizers; solid mineral fuels;
petroleum and all hydrocarbons—solid, liquid, or gaseous.

In the nation is likewise vested the ownership of the waters of territorial seas to the extent and in the terms fixed by the law of nations;
those of lakes and inlets of bays; those of interior lakes of natural formation which are directly connected with flowing waters; those of principal rivers or tributaries from the points at which their courses become

permanently identifiable to their mouths, whether they flow to the sea or cross two or more States; those of intermittent streams which traverse two or more States in their main body; the waters of rivers, streams, or ravines, when they bound the national territory or that of the States; waters extracted from mines; and the beds and banks of the lakes and streams hereinbefore mentioned, to the extent fixed by law. Any other stream of water not comprised within the foregoing enumeration shall be considered as an integral part of the private property through which it flows; but the development of the waters when they pass from one landed property to another shall be considered of public utility and shall be subject to the provisions prescribed by the States.

In the cases to which the two foregoing paragraphs refer, the ownership of the nation is inalienable and may not be lost by prescription; concessions shall be granted by the Federal Government to provide parties or civil or commercial corporations organized under the laws of Mexico, only on condition that said resources be regularly developed, and on the further condition that the legal provisions be observed.

Legal capacity to acquire ownership of lands and waters of the nation shall be governed by the following provisions:

I. Only Mexicans by birth or naturalization and Mexican companies have the right to acquire ownership in lands, waters, and their appurtenances, or to obtain concessions to develop mines, waters, or mineral fuels in the Republic of Mexico. The nation may grant the same right to foreigners, provided they agree before the department of foreign affairs to be considered Mexicans in respect to such property, and accordingly not to invoke the protection of their Governments in respect to the same, under penalty, in case of breach, of forfeiture to the nation of property so acquired. Within a zone of 100 kilometers from the frontiers, and of 50 kilometers from the seacoast no foreigner shall under any conditions acquire direct ownership of lands and waters.

II. The religious associations known as churches, irrespective of creed, shall in no case have legal capacity to acquire, hold, or administer real property or loans made on such real property; all such real property or loans as may be at present held by the said religious associations either on their own behalf or through third parties shall vest in the nation. . . . Places of public worship are the property of the nation, as represented by the Federal Government, which shall determine which of them may continue to be devoted to their present purposes. . . .

IV. Commercial stock companies may not acquire, hold, or administer rural properties. Companies of this nature which may be organized to develop any manufacturing, mining, petroleum, or other industry, excepting only agricultural industries, may acquire, hold, or administer lands only in an area absolutely necessary for their establishments or adequate to serve the purposes indicated, which the executive of the union or of the State in each case shall determine.

V. The banks duly organized under the laws governing institutions of credit may make mortgage loans on rural and urban property in accordance with the provisions of the said laws, but they may not own or administer more real property than that absolutely necessary for their direct purposes; and they may furthermore hold temporarily for the brief term fixed by law such real property as may be judicially adjudicated to them in execution proceedings.

VI. Properties held in common by coowners, hamlets situated on private property, pueblos, tribal congregations and other settlements which, as a matter of fact or law, conserve their communal character, shall have legal capacity to enjoy in common the waters, woods and lands belonging to them, or which may have been or shall be restored to them according to the law of January 6, 1915, until such time as the manner of making the division exclusively of the lands shall be determined by law.

VII. Excepting the corporations to which Clauses III, IV, V and VI hereof refer no other civil corporation may hold or administer on its own behalf real estate or mortgage loans derived therefrom, with the single exception of buildings designed directly and immediately for the purposes of the institution. The States, the Federal district and the Territories as well as the municipalities throughout the Republic shall enjoy full legal capacity to acquire and hold all real estate necessary for public services.

The Federal and State laws shall determine within their respective jurisdictions those cases in which the occupation of private property is to be considered of public utility; and in accordance with the said laws the administrative authorities shall make the corresponding declaration. The amount fixed as compensation for the expropriated property shall be based on the sum at which the said property shall be valued for fiscal purposes in the . . . revenue offices, whether this value be that manifested by the owner or merely impliedly accepted by reason of the payment of his taxes on such a basis, to which basis there shall be added 10 per cent. . . .

During the next constitutional term the Congress and the State legislatures shall enact laws within their respective jurisdictions for the purpose of carrying out the division of large landed estates subject to the following conditions:

(*a*) In each State and Territory there shall be fixed the maximum area of land which any one individual or legally organized corporation may own.

(*b*) The excess of the area fixed shall be subdivided by the owner within the period set by the laws of the respective locality; and these subdivisions shall be offered for sale on such conditions as the respective governments shall approve, in accordance with the said laws.

(*c*) If the owner shall refuse to make the subdivision, this shall be carried out by the local government by means of expropriation proceedings.

(*d*) The value of the subdivisions shall be paid in annual amounts sufficient to amortize the principal and interest within a period of not less than 20 years, during which the person acquiring them may not alienate them. The rate of interest shall not exceed 5 per cent per annum.

(*e*) The owner shall be bound to receive special bonds to guarantee the payment of the property expropriated. With this end in view the Congress shall issue a law authorizing the States to issue bonds to meet their agrarian obligations.

(*f*) The local laws will govern the extent of family estate, determining what property will constitute the same on the basis of its inalienability; it shall not be subject to attachment nor to any charge.

All contracts and concessions made by former governments from and after the year 1876 which shall have resulted in the monopoly of lands, waters, and natural resources of the nation by a single individual or corporation, are declared subject to revision, and the executive is authorized to declare those null and void which seriously prejudice the public interest.

32

CONSTITUTIONAL CONVENTION

The Constitution of 1917: The Labor Provisions of Article 123

1917

Article 123 was, perhaps, the most radical provision of the Constitution of 1917, for it redressed the treatment of workers in terms of both the conditions of their labor and their equality before the law. Note that section VII provides for equal pay for equal work regardless of sex or nationality. Section XVII establishes the right of workers to strike.

ART. 123.—The Congress and the State legislatures shall make laws relative to labor, with due regard for the needs of each region of the Republic and in conformity with the following principles, and these principles and laws shall govern the labor of skilled and unskilled workmen, employees, domestic servants and artisans, and in general every contract of labor.

I. Eight hours shall be the maximum limit of a day's work.

II. The maximum limit of night work shall be seven hours. Unhealthy and dangerous occupations are forbidden to all women and to children under 16 years of age. Night work in factories is likewise forbidden to women and to children under 16 years of age, nor shall they be employed in commercial establishments after 10 o'clock at night.

III. The maximum limit of a day's work for children over 12 and under 16 years of age shall be six hours. The work of children under 12 years of age can not be made the object of a contract.

IV. Every workman shall enjoy at least one day's rest for every six days' work.

V. Women shall not perform any physical work requiring considerable physical effort during the three months immediately preceding parturition; during the month following parturition they shall necessarily

---

From "Political Constitution of the United States of Mexico: Title VI.—Of Labor and Social Welfare," in United States Senate, Committee on Foreign Relations, *Investigation of Mexican Affairs* (Washington, D.C.: Government Printing Office, 1920), 2:3146–47.

enjoy a period of rest and shall receive their salaries or wages in full and retain their employment and the rights they may have acquired under their contracts. During the period of lactation they shall enjoy two extraordinary daily periods of rest of one-half hour each in order to nurse their children.

VI. The minimum wage to be received by a workman shall be that considered sufficient, according to the conditions prevailing in the respective region of the country to satisfy the normal needs of the life of the workman, his education, and his lawful pleasures, considering him as the head of a family. In all agricultural, commercial, manufacturing, or mining enterprises the workmen shall have the right to participate in the profits in the manner fixed in Clause IX of this article.

VII. The same compensation shall be paid for the same work without regard to sex or nationality.

VIII. The minimum wage shall be exempt from attachment, set-off, or discount.

IX. The determination of the minimum wage and of the rate of profit-sharing described in clause VI shall be made by special commissions to be appointed in each municipality and to be subordinated to the central board of conciliation to be established in each state.

X. All wages shall be paid in legal currency and shall not be paid in merchandise orders, counters, or any other representative token with which it is sought to substitute money.

XI. When owing to special circumstances it becomes necessary to increase the working hours there shall be paid as wages for the over-time 100 per cent more than those fixed for regular time. In no case shall the overtime exceed three hours nor continue for more than three consecutive days; and no women of whatever age nor boys under 16 years of age may engage in overtime work.

XII. In every agricultural, industrial, mining, or similar class of work employers are bound to furnish their workmen comfortable and sanitary dwelling places, for which they may charge rents not exceeding one-half of 1 per cent per month of the assessed value of the properties. They shall likewise establish schools, dispensaries, and other services necessary to the community. If the factories are located within inhabited places and more than 100 persons are employed therein, the first of the above-mentioned conditions shall be complied with.

XIII. Furthermore, there shall be set aside in these labor centers, whenever their population exceeds 200 inhabitants, a space of land not less than 5,000 square meters for the establishment of public markets, and the construction of buildings designed for municipal service and places of amusement. No saloons or gambling houses shall be permitted in such labor centers.

XIV. Employers shall be liable for labor accidents and occupational diseases arising from work; therefore employers shall pay the proper indemnity, according to whether death or merely temporary or permanent disability has ensued, in accordance with the provisions of law. This liability shall remain in force even though the employer contract for the work through an agent.

XV. Employers shall be bound to observe in the installation of their establishments all the provisions of law regarding hygiene and sanitation and to adopt adequate measures to prevent accidents due to the use of machinery, tools, and working materials, as well as to organize work in such a manner as to assure the greatest guaranties possible for the health and lives of workmen compatible with the nature of the work, under penalties which the law shall determine.

XVI. Workmen and employers shall have the right to unite for the defense of their respective interests, by forming syndicates, unions, etc.

XVII. The law shall recognize the right of workmen and employers to strike and to suspend work.

XVIII. Strikes shall be lawful when by the employment of peaceful means they shall aim to bring about a balance between the various factors of production and to harmonize the rights of capital and labor. . . .

XIX. Lockouts shall only be lawful when the excess of production shall render it necessary to shut down in order to maintain prices reasonably above the cost of production, subject to the approval of the board of conciliation and arbitration.

XX. Differences or disputes between capital and labor shall be submitted for settlement to a board of conciliation and arbitration to consist of an equal number of representatives of the workmen and of the employers and of one representative of the Government. . . .

XXIII. Claims of workmen for salaries or wages accrued during the past year and other indemnity claims shall be preferred over any other claims in cases of bankruptcy or execution proceedings.

XXIV. Debts contracted by workmen in favor of their employers or their employers' associates, subordinates, or agents, may only be charged against the workmen themselves, and in no case and for no reason collected from the members of his family. Nor shall such debts be paid by the taking of more than the entire wages of the workman for any one month.

XXV. No fee shall be charged for finding work for workmen by municipal offices, employment bureaus, or other public or private agencies.

33

ROSALIE EVANS

Letters from Mexico

1920–1923

Rosalie Caden was a young American woman who accompanied her parents to Mexico in 1896. There she met and married Harry Evans, an Englishman, whose father had earned considerable wealth under the Díaz regime. Originally a banker, Evans bought a run-down estate, the Hacienda San Pedro Coxtocan, in Puebla. The Evanses rebuilt the property and made it into a showplace. Revolutionaries ransacked the hacienda in 1910, forcing the owners to reside in Mexico City for the next three years. From 1913 to 1917, they split their time between the United States and England. In 1917, while on a business trip to Mexico, Harry took ill and died. Early in 1918, Rosalie returned to Mexico to recover and restore her property. For the next five years, she defended her hacienda against local politicians who coveted it. She was murdered there in 1923. Hers is a story of the dark side of the Revolution, with corruption underlying a veneer of reform. The selections here are from her last three years in Mexico.

MEXICO CITY,
JUNE 30, 1920.

I am only just back from the hacienda. The creatures stopped the threshing again by throwing a piece of iron in the motor. Really, I must have told you that, no? Well, I heard an awful uproar and men all gesticulating and pointing to the broken machine. I never thought I would be sorry for an engine, but it had seventeen teeth lying on the ground and the main shaft smashed. Well, I had to go to Puebla again, the third time, but I finally got it straightened and I did not have to pay. I have not finished the threshing yet, but simply could not stay away any longer, for many things need my attention here.

I have to ship three more cars of wheat and put in a new partition of water . . . and I am trying to make Lozano draw up the document. The most important business is the water. I thought the Indians were up to

From Rosalie Evans, *The Rosalie Evans Letters from Mexico* (Indianapolis: Bobbs-Merrill, 1926), 134–37, 194–98.

mischief, they have been so docile, and I found at Lozano's office that a new scheme had been hatched to divide the hacienda, all of which will have to be fought out again. Of course the Indians are instigated by government officials.

SAN PEDRO,
SEPTEMBER 25, 1920.

. . . This morning . . . the gardener told me that Francisco Rosas, he who leads the Bolsheviki of the village, was out with his men dividing the land and had driven the good Indians off. I immediately went to see what I should or could do with only one man. . . . As I left the avenue and turned into the field I saw about thirty men walking slowly, led by Rosas, measuring off my field (plowed now by the good Indians). That did not rouse me, until the man with me said: "See them gathering stones to throw at you." Each had a big stone in his hand. That did make me angry, but still I felt quite equal to them all. Rosas answered, when I asked what orders he had to divide the land, that he had left them at home and did not mean to show them to me—where were mine? I replied that I needed none—the ground belonged to me and to leave it instantly or I should have to send for soldiers. "Run and get them," answered he, and went on measuring. That is where my rage got me. My horse is a little darling. I made her plunge about, scattering the men right and left, while I drew my pistol. One man saw I was in earnest and lifted a large stone to throw at me, seeing my pistol caught in the holster, but I got my finger on the trigger and pointed at the broad breast of Rosas: "If that man throws that stone I'll shoot you." The stone fell, but not in my direction. The mare seemed to understand and stood quite still and my hand was as steady—my trembling hand—as I never dreamed it could be. I said: "I need no soldiers to do my work. If you plow this ground without an order from the government I shall fire on the first man who dares it."

All of which sounds very bold, but I felt calm and quite sure they would do nothing to harm me.

They tried to parley, but I refused to hear them. "If you have an order," I said, "bring it to the house and show it to me, and I shall let you work."

They replied: "Very well, we shall bring our order."

And I marched them off my ground. . . .

. . . You could see they had intended a desperate stand, but had not calculated on my drawing my pistol. They were both humiliated and furious.

I can not tell the result, the story has spread I know. My kitchen is silent, the men working pass me quietly and watchfully—the older ones have a lurking smile—but I have talked it over with no one but you.

I came home, washed my hair . . . — if we are to meet death to-night, we shall at least be clean, and we all ate dinner cheerfully. I mean to keep the place.

SAN PEDRO COXTOCAN,
MARCH 12, 1923.

. . . I had just returned from San Pedro and mailed you a society letter of dinners and functions and I think mentioned a red army of ragged men marching past.

I had barely reached Mexico City when Iago began informing me they were taking up all the ancient milestones marking the limits or boundaries of the hacienda and putting new ones down, giving the entire place over to the people — all that they promised not to do. I told him not to interfere, for you see this is a fight for the owner, not just an outrage by the people, but *government* orders. So long as there is an unrepealed presidential decree confiscating a property the owner is at the mercy of every petty official. Obregon, aware of this, trusts to some underling to carry out his orders, or rid him of the obstacle.

I wrote, telephoned and tried in every way to get De Negri,[1] but was not received. I knew some force was acting against me again with Obregon. It was useless going to Mr. Cummins[2] — he has done his all for the moment — unless I get killed. I want to outwit them and am bending all my energies to that end. I finally got Pani, and said if they did not give me support I should go to the hacienda and knock down their "monuments" and put the old ones back. He begged me not to go until he spoke again with De Negri. Result: Last Wednesday I got a letter from his secretary to the governor of Puebla, saying to assist me, and all orders would be given by telegraph. I got to Puebla Wednesday afternoon; the governor received me. He said *no* orders had been sent. I told him I should have to go at once to San Pedro and knock down the monuments. That, they don't want, for I might get killed and so call attention to the robbery. . . .

Not being here you can't follow all the details, excitements and exasperations, broken engagements, etc., but after my first interview with the governor and his youthful, ignorant and dishonest staff, I possessed my soul in Job-like patience. . . .

When I reached San Pedro ten of my best and kindliest Indians were waiting to see if I had *orders* from Obregon against the *agrarios*.[3] They

---

[1] Ramón De Negri, secretary of agriculture in the Obregón government.
[2] Mr. Cummins, chargé d'affaires at the British embassy in Mexico City.
[3] *agrarios*: Peasants who sought land redistribution.

had put red flags all over my boundaries, or rather on the new stones, and would bury me under them, if I took them down. I told the Indians the truth. Puebla had orders to protect me, but was refusing to execute them. Such a position could not last. They went off. Then I went to see the outrage, on horseback, with Diego and Iago—both armed. I didn't want them shot or arrested, but when I saw the red flags I pulled them down. The last they had put on a mound too high for me and not room on top for the horse to stand—only to dash up on one side and down the other. Before they could stop me I forced the horse up, caught the flag-staff in passing and with the weight of the horse broke it off! It was really exhilarating—. . . . I have never stormed a citadel or captured a flag before. . . .

The *agrarios* fired on me, but even that only added excitement and pleasure. I got off with the banner and blocked off Diego and Iago and would not let them return the agrarians' fire, as their bullets fell short. Nor would I run, but walked the horse slowly back to the hacienda—with Diego and Iago keeping their guns ready if they attacked us. We planned to charge them with a volley if they came near, but they never did. . . .

This morning I used a little of the wisdom of the serpent and again scattered telegrams to the highest in Mexico saying: "No protection was given me. Puebla did not obey orders. Fired on, etc. Could not leave hacienda until my people and property were protected."

SAN PEDRO,
MARCH 14, 1923.

A weary time since I wrote you and never a minute in peace. This is a curious minute to choose, but I am clear-minded, as always, when I have made a decision. I'll continue where I left off. In the morning several of my men came to knock down the new boundary-stones and fight for me. On reflection, I would not let them, for in Mexico City they would have a right to say, if some got killed, that they had promised to help me and I would not give them time. My trouble is this dark inquisitorial Puebla. Yesterday I came here (Puebla) having received a telegram from the *jefe*[4] David, brother of the governor, that he had orders from Mexico City to call the people before me and make them change the monuments. I spent an hour or so yesterday afternoon and was not received—this morning, an hour, when an official I know murmured: "Waste no more time here. Go to Mexico City." So I shall see what can be done there. I take the morning train.

---

[4]*jefe*: The chief or local political boss.

7

International Ramifications

Though fought primarily as a domestic civil war, the Mexican Revolution attracted enormous attention in the United States and Europe. Foreign entrepreneurs and corporations had invested more than a billion dollars in Mexican railroads, mines, farms, and industries, and their home governments sought to protect their interests. American investors had the most to lose, followed by the British.

Foreign investments, however, were only part of the story. The United States was deeply involved in the rebels' machinations before and during the initial stages of the Revolution, led by Francisco Madero. Its diplomats were entangled in plotting Madero's assassination in 1913. The United States intervened militarily with considerable force in 1914, occupying Mexico's two major ports, Veracruz and Tampico, both on the Gulf coast. In 1916, President Woodrow Wilson dispatched an expeditionary force into northern Mexico in pursuit of Pancho Villa, who had staged a one-day raid on Columbus, New Mexico. Three years later, U.S. troops made a brief incursion into Mexico to disperse a contingent of Villa's troops that had captured and occupied Ciudad Juárez, just across the border from El Paso, Texas.

The Europeans had diplomatic as well as economic interests in Mexico. Most notably, in early 1915 the German government, anticipating the United States' entry into World War I on the side of Britain, France, and Russia, proposed that Mexico invade its northern neighbor. When this so-called Zimmermann telegram became public, it helped push the United States toward war with Germany.

After the second U.S. invasion, in 1916, and after the hardest fighting of the Revolution had ended, foreign governments remained worried about the new constitution adopted in 1917. It provided that the ownership of subsoil rights (oil and minerals) would revert to the nation and that all private property was subject to expropriation for the good of the people. Foreign petroleum and mining companies and foreign landowners fiercely resisted attempts to implement these radical measures.

34

HENRY LANE WILSON

Ten Tragic Days

1913

Henry Lane Wilson was U.S. ambassador to Mexico from 1909 to 1913. Previously, he had been U.S. minister to Chile and Belgium. He worked tirelessly against Madero, plotting to overthrow the president with reactionaries Félix Díaz and Victoriano Huerta during the Ten Tragic Days in February 1913. His disdain for Madero was evidenced by his unwillingness to intervene to save the deposed president's life. In this excerpt from his memoir, Wilson defends his activities during the Ten Tragic Days. He maintains that he consulted with Díaz and Huerta in an effort to end the horrific destruction and bloodshed in Mexico City as the armies of Madero, then led by Huerta, and Díaz fought in the streets of the capital. He quite clearly admits to having helped frame the agreement that brought the generals into an alliance that toppled Madero.

On the seventh day of the bombardment, deeply concerned for the safety of many Americans remaining within the firing lines and who could not be rescued, I went to the national palace . . . for the purpose of procuring from General Huerta an armistice, during the continuation of which foreigners might be removed to places of safety. Upon our arrival at the palace, much to our regret, because we hoped for prompt action from Huerta, we were taken to see the President whom we had not asked to see, and it was only by insistence that we were permitted to have an interview with General Huerta. . . . I asked (1) that the military dispositions of the government should be made so as to avoid firing at the Citadel over the residential quarter; (2) that the American embassy should be treated as a humanitarian establishment and a free zone established around it; (3) that the government should unite with an American committee in establishing centres for the distribution of bread to the poor; (4) that federal soldiers on American buildings which

From Henry Lane Wilson, *Diplomatic Episodes in Mexico, Belgium and Chile* (New York: Doubleday, Page, 1927), 259–61, 279–82.

had been made places of refuge should be removed; (5) that an armistice of three hours should be given to enable our rescue committee to take starving Americans and other foreigners out of the firing line; (6) that an armistice of twelve hours should be given to enable foreigners to leave the city by train. These demands were finally agreed to by General Huerta and the President. . . .

The establishment of the armistice and the subsequent rescue work by the embassy committees were distinctly humanitarian acts. . . . Some fifteen hundred . . . people, mostly Americans, some of them in a starving condition, were removed from the danger zone. . . .

Later . . . I determined that I must take a decisive step on my own responsibility to bring about a restoration of order. This was the situation: Two hostile armies were in possession of the capital and all civil authority had disappeared; sinister bands of looters and robbers were beginning to appear in many of the streets of the capital; starving men, women, and children were parading in many public thoroughfares. Some 35,000 foreigners who, as developed during the bombardment, seemed to rely upon the embassy for protection, were at the mercy of the mob or exposed to indiscriminate firing which might at any moment begin between the forces of General Huerta and General Felix Diaz, thus reinvolving the lives and property of non-combatants. Without having conferred with any one, I decided to ask Generals Huerta and Diaz to come to the embassy, which, as neutral ground, would guarantee good faith and protection, for a consultation. My object was to have them enter into an agreement for the suspension of hostilities and for joint submission to the federal congress. . . .

I lost no time in bringing the two generals together in the embassy library whither, to my dismay, they brought a number of retainers and advisers. These so-called advisers soon engaged in wordy conflicts betokening unknown duration and infinite possibilities. This was not the purpose of the meeting, and I was finally obliged to ask all but General Huerta and General Diaz and my clerk, d'Antin, to withdraw. I then said to the two generals that I had called them together solely for the purpose of terminating the conditions which had existed in Mexico for the last ten days, conditions which had inflicted incredible suffering on the population of the city, had involved the destruction of ten thousand lives and a vast amount of public and private property; that these conditions must continue indefinitely unless the two belligerents arranged their differences and submitted to Congress, the only existing representative of the people. Three times, when the discussion was broken off, I entered the room and with appeals to their reason and patriotism induced them to continue. Finally, to force a decision, I said to them that unless they brought about peace the demand by European powers for intervention might become too strong to be resisted by the Washington government. This had the desired effect, and at one o'clock in the morning, the agreement was signed, deposited in the embassy safe, and a proclamation announcing the cessation of hostilities was issued. During this conference, exceedingly dramatic in some of its phases, a throng of anxious thousands surrounded the embassy. Within there was subdued but animated discussion, a battle of conflicting interests; without, the vast throng waited expectantly, patiently, for the announcement of a decision which so closely concerned their lives, their property, and their country. When it was finally announced that by the agreement of all parties an arrangement had been reached, and that with the authority of Congress General Huerta was to be provisional president and General Diaz was to be free to pursue his candidacy for the presidency, the news ran like wildfire through the city and was welcomed with universal rejoicing. That night thirty thousand people paraded through the streets of Mexico City giving thanks for peace and to the American government for having been instrumental in bringing it about. President Wilson considered the part played by the embassy as an intrusion in the domestic affairs of Mexico; persons who rest pleasantly by the home fires sometimes have curious conceptions of what the conduct of a public officer should be under critical and dangerous conditions. After years of mature consideration I do not hesitate to say that if I were confronted with the same situation under the same conditions I should take precisely the same course.

The consummation of this arrangement I regard as the most successful and far-reaching of the difficult work I was called upon to perform during the revolution, in that it stopped further effusion of blood, allowed the population of the city to resume its usual peaceful occupations, and led finally to the creation of a provisional government which rapidly restored peace throughout the republic.

35

EDITH O'SHAUGHNESSY

A Diplomat's Wife

1914

Edith O'Shaughnessy was the wife of Nelson O'Shaughnessy, the chargé d'affaires (second-in-command) at the U.S. embassy in Mexico City during the Madero and Huerta regimes. She provides in her memoirs, A Diplomat's Wife in Mexico *and* Diplomatic Days *(both decidedly pro-Huerta), a foreigner's view of the events taking place. She is, of course, mainly concerned about the damage to American property and the safety of U.S. citizens in Mexico. In this excerpt from* Diplomatic Days, *she subtly pokes fun at Madero.*

NOVEMBER 7TH.

Late yesterday afternoon ex-President de la Barra, accompanied by his family and the staff of his mission, left for Vera Cruz to take *La Champagne* for France, *en route* to Rome. There was a great demonstration at his departure. The *Corps Diplomatique* was out in full force, and all Mexico besides, it seemed, as we got down to the station, around which mounted soldiery with difficulty kept a free space, pressing the crowd back to let in the carriages and motors, one by one.

The most interesting thing about it all, to me, was the group that at one time formed itself on the rear platform of the special train—President Madero, ex-President de la Barra, and Orozco, the military genius of the moment, the type of the trio so distinct as they stood there. Orozco is a very tall man, head and shoulders over the other two, the northern Mexico ranchero type—prominent nose, high cheek bones, with a dark mustache that doesn't at all conceal a cruel, determined mouth.

De la Barra, international, immaculately dressed, suave, smiling, was entirely the diplomat departing on a special mission, showing no trace of the difficult and anxious months of office.

Edith O'Shaughnessy, *Diplomatic Days* (New York: Harper and Brothers, 1917), 150–51, 252.

Between these two stood the President of but a few hours, with his broad, high, speculative forehead, his dreamy, impractical eyes and kindly smile—"one man with a dream at pleasure."

Madero is naturally generous toward his enemies, of which the crops, however, hourly increase. He is averse to shedding blood, but I sigh for the difficulties of his position, between various upper and nether millstones, with the destinies of fifteen millions of people like to be ground between.

All the *revolucionarios* who came in with him seem to have dreamed some of his vague dreams, to which they add, however, very determined desires to settle in comfortable nests built by others on the extraordinarily simple plan of "see a home, take it." The upper classes, what little one sees of them, shake their heads, cast up their eyes, and throw out their hands. It's all very uncertain, but most interesting to a lady from the temperate zone. . . .

APRIL 17

. . . [The U.S. Embassy] call[s] categoric attention to the enormous destruction of American property, ever on the increase in Mexico, and the taking of American life, contrary to the usages of civilized nations.

The United States expects and demands that American life and property within the Republic of Mexico be justly and adequately protected, and will hold Mexico and the Mexicans responsible for all wanton and illegal acts sacrificing or endangering them.

We further insist that the rules and principles accepted by civilized nations as controlling their actions in time of war shall be observed. Any deviation from such a course, any maltreatment of any American citizen, will be deeply resented by the American government and people, and must be fully answered for by the Mexican people. The shooting of the unfortunate, misguided Thomas Fountain by Orozco (said T.F. was having a little fling seeing life, and death, too, with the Federal forces) is deplored. Orozco "answers back" that naturally he executed Fountain, who was "fighting in the enemy's army." Several Americans, employed on the Mexican railways, have also been murdered by the revolutionists.

The Mexican reply, drawn up by the long-headed, very prudent Don Pedro Lascurain, the new Minister for Foreign Affairs, says Mexico finds itself in the painful position of not recognizing the right of our government to make the various admonitions . . . since these are not based on any incident chargeable to the Mexican government, or which could signify that it had departed from an observance of the principles and practices of international law.

36

WALTER HINES PAGE

The Zimmermann Telegram

1917

In January 1917, German foreign minister Arthur Zimmermann sent a secret message to the government of Venustiano Carranza, then the First Chief of the Constitutionalists, proposing an alliance between Germany and Mexico against the United States. The Germans hoped to prevent the United States from entering the war in Europe on the side of Britain, France, and Russia. When the British made the telegram public, the ensuing furor helped push the United States into the war. The German proposal, foolish as it may have been in retrospect, put Carranza in a difficult position. He could not afford to alienate the United States. Although President Wilson had officially recognized Carranza's government, he had considerable reservations about Carranza's treatment of American companies operating in Mexico. Carranza's best strategy, then, was to ignore the matter. He never acknowledged or replied to Zimmermann.

LONDON, FEBRUARY 24, 1917, 1 P.M.

[RECEIVED 8:30 P.M.]

February 24, 8 a.m. For the President and the Secretary of State. Balfour[1] has handed me the text of a cipher telegram from Zimmermann, German Secretary of State for Foreign Affairs, to the German Minister to Mexico, which was sent via Washington and relayed . . . on January 19. . . .

We intend to begin on the 1st of February unrestricted submarine warfare. We shall endeavor in spite of this to keep the United States of America neutral. In the event of this not succeeding, we make Mexico a proposal of alliance on the following basis: make war together, make

[1]Arthur James Balfour, the British foreign minister.

From "The Ambassador in Great Britain (Page) to the Secretary of State," telegram, February 24, 1917, in U.S. Department of State, *Papers Relating to the Foreign Relations of the United States, 1917*, suppl. 1: *The World War* (Washington, D.C.: Government Printing Office, 1931), 147.

peace together, generous financial support and an understanding on our part that Mexico is to reconquer the lost territory in Texas, New Mexico, and Arizona. The settlement in detail is left to you. You will inform the President of the above most secretly as soon as the outbreak of war with the United States of America is certain and add the suggestion that he should, on his own initiative, invite Japan to immediate adherence and at the same time mediate between Japan and ourselves. Please call the President's attention to the fact that the ruthless employment of our submarines now offers the prospect of compelling England in a few months to make peace. Signed, Zimmermann.

The receipt of this information has so greatly exercised the British Government that they have lost no time in communicating it to me to transmit to you, in order that our Government may be able without delay to make such disposition as may be necessary in view of the threatened invasion of our territory.

37

CHARLES F. SIMON

Testimony in Support of His Claim against the Republic of Mexico

1919

Senator Albert B. Fall was an investor in Mexico and a confidant of both the powerful Terrazas family of Chihuahua and the dictator Porfirio Díaz. Fall was one of the most vocal proponents of U.S. intervention in Mexico. He headed a subcommittee of the Senate Committee on Foreign Relations that began investigating conditions in Mexico in late 1919. Witnesses testifying before the subcommittee painted a picture of the destruction of American property during the upheaval. These witnesses often exaggerated the extent of their holdings and the damages sustained. As U.S. secretary of the interior, Fall later became involved in the famous Teapot Dome scandal of the Harding administration and was the first cabinet member to be sent to jail. In this excerpt from testimony before

From "Memorial of Charles F. Simon in Support of His Claim against the Republic of Mexico," in United States Senate, Committee on Foreign Relations, *Investigation of Mexican Affairs* (Washington, D.C.: Government Printing Office, 1920), 2:3294–95.

Fall's subcommittee, coffee plantation owner Charles F. Simon details his claim against the Mexican government.

I, Charles F. Simon, claimant, am a citizen of the United States of America. I was born October 2, 1861, in the city of St. Louis, State of Missouri, and resided in that city until about 20 years ago, when I purchased about 1,800 acres of land in the State of Vera Cruz, Mexico, about 40 miles from the city of Jalapa. This land lies in two adjacent valleys, one known as "Clarin," one as "Rincon Negros." I planted on these lands 300,000 coffee trees, cleared pastures, made roads and fences. I built a residence for my family, also houses for workmen, stables, waterworks, drying grounds for coffee, and a machinery house in which I installed a complete outfit of modern machinery for the treatment of coffee. By 1914 I had in successful and profitable operation my coffee plantations with a full complement of workmen, who were well treated, well paid, and contented. They had the privilege without cost, of corn land, bean land, and pasture. I cared for them when they were sick, and in every way treated them with consideration. I was encouraged in this enterprise by the then existing Government.

On or about the 23d of April, 1914, the Mexicans living near the property entered my residence, situated in Clarin, by force, broke open two locked desks and several locked cupboards, took all my papers, title deeds, accounts, and some money, breaking some of the furniture. After the American troops left Vera Cruz I secured the title deeds to the property, but not my accounts, papers, money, etc.

We now come to the year 1916. Senor Caranza was in power and the district in which I lived swarmed with his opponents, something like 800 armed men. They rode around in small bands, living largely off the people like myself who had houses, beds, and food. Fifty of them would ride up to my house and other ranches of Americans at nightfall, and we would be forced to put them up for the night and often longer, feeding the men and horses. They go away, of course, without paying, sometimes taking saddles, blankets, and what money one is forced to let them have. In fact one is completely at their mercy, and they play with him as a cat does a mouse, all this notwithstanding the Mexican Federal Government was fully apprised of the situation by appeals from myself and others.

In April, 1916, Gen. Cejudo, who was the chief of the rebels in my district, took over my property and used my residence as military headquarters. I lived in Jalapa some 40 miles away, which city was within the control of the Federal authorities. I wrote to Gen. Cejudo protesting over his action in taking over my property. He replied that he regrets it, but he is obeying superior orders, and will give finally a full report to our consul in Vera Cruz, which was never done. The result is my foreman and workmen, with their families, were forced to leave the place and the ranch was abandoned to the mercy of the rebels. Before they left my foreman, Felipe Diaz, and my storekeeper, Candido Carretero, made an inventory of the contents of my residence, also an inventory of the houses and machinery, etc., which I file with this paper, together with their affidavits. The rebels took possession of all the coffee that was on the ranch, also all other articles that they could use to advantage, and finally completely wrecked the contents of my residence.

Those articles of furniture which they could not well carry off they destroyed. They stabled horses in the parlor and generally defiled the house. The garden of several acres which surrounds the house they have used for a corral for mules and the valuable plants were completely ruined. In December, 1916, my foreman received word that the rebels would allow him to return. So he wired me to the United States where I was then living. I replied by wire to take full force of men and start work cleaning up the property. I knew that if this was not done that the entire plantation would be ruined. If a coffee plantation is not kept free from weeds, the trees deteriorate rapidly and soon die. The growth of weeds in the Tropics is excessive and the plantings must be cleaned from four to six times each year. As we had been forced to abandon the property the previous spring, and in the meantime the rainy season had come and gone, the coffee plants were smothered in weeds. My foreman gathered all the workmen in the district and started to clean up the plantation, in the meantime following behind with the coffee pickers. The coffee crop comes on about the 1st of November and lasts until March. Before the 1st of November a plantation should be cleaned and ready to be picked. I knew that it would be impossible to pick the crop on account of the fact of our getting possession of the plantation so late in the season. However, I thought that I might be able to get some of it to help to pay for at least part of the expenses of the weeding of the plantation. We cropped in the spring of 1916, 107,456 kilos, whereas in 1917, owing to the fact that the rebels had my plantation in their possession and had run off all of my workmen, we were only able to crop 18,446 kilos, thereby losing 89,100 kilos. I have stated that the 1916 crop was 107,456 kilos.

As a fact, we were unable to crop all of it, being disturbed so much by those roving, armed bands, so that we lost about 23,000 kilos, which dropped from the trees and could not be recovered. I make a claim for the loss of the crop this 1917 season and base the loss on the difference between what was actually picked in 1916 and in 1917. All taxes have been paid by me to the Mexican Government up to January 1, 1917. My ranch is still in the power of the rebels. They have an officer living on my plantation. I make a claim for the deterioration of the value of the plantations through being left abandoned. A plantation so left in the Tropics reverts in a short time to a wilderness of growth, killing off all artificial plantings and ruining the labor of years. I have claimed 15 per cent of the total plantings. In my itemized account I have called the total planting only 255,000 trees, whereas I have stated in this report that I had planted 300,000. This is owing to the fact that 45,000 trees had been abandoned because they had been planted in badly exposed places. I make a claim for the damage done to the houses. These left open to the wind, rain, animals, for any length of time soon go to pieces. This damage is considerable, and I have placed a conservative amount for which I believe they can be replaced or patched up as good as they were. I make claims for articles stolen; also horses, mules, cattle, coffee; for the destruction of contents of my residence and garden. All this is shown by affidavits made by one who was living on the place and filed herewith. I submit some receipts for a portion of the stolen property, as we secured all of these we possibly could. In all cases the amounts representing costs are set down with strict justice, and the amounts claimed are less rather than more than the actual damage sustained. The Mexican Federal Government has collected taxes, but has failed to afford me protection. The damages I now claim are what I have suffered up to May, 1917.

The conditions in the district have continued about the same since that time. The rebels are still in possession of my ranch; they dominate the neighborhood and the Government has failed to suppress them. I have spent large sums of money in attempting to regain and operate my ranch. A German living on adjoining property has never been molested. The policy of our Government has been misunderstood by the Mexican people and the American subjects have suffered in consequence. My house was completely furnished for occupation by myself and family, consisting of my wife and three children. The furniture included my silverware, cut glass, china, general furniture, rugs, a valuable library, pictures, bric-a-brac, etc., all of which was taken away or destroyed. I attach hereto as Exhibit A a rough itemized account of my property destroyed and damaged, together with the fair cash value thereof, also incidental expenses incurred by me. Such account is correct according to my best knowledge and belief. . . .

On account of conditions existing since May, 1917, I have been unable to visit my ranch or to operate it successfully. I have suffered many losses since May, 1917, but shall ask leave to submit proof of same later. My property is practically ruined and I am debarred from the country.

I make this claim in behalf of myself as owner of the property referred to in this memorial. I am and was when this claim originated a citizen of the United States. At the present time I am domiciled in the city of New York. When this claim originated, I was domiciled in the city of Jalapa, Mexico. I was never a subject of the Republic of Mexico, and never took an oath of allegiance to the Government thereof. The entire amount of this claim belongs to me and did when it had its origin. I have never received any sum of money or other quivalent or indemnification for the whole or any part of the loss and injury upon which this claim is founded. I am 56 years old.

At present I am engaged in business at 225 Fifth Avenue, in New York City, having been compelled to abandon my Mexican property as stated above, with no prospect of being able to rescue and restore it.

38

MARION LETCHER

American, British, and Mexican Investment in Mexico

1911

As the Revolution erupted in 1911, Marion Letcher, U.S. Consul in Chihuahua, Mexico, compiled an assessment of the wealth of Mexico and the extent of foreign investment. According to his report, foreign companies and individual entrepreneurs invested heavily in Mexico during the Díaz era. They controlled more than two-thirds of the nation's wealth. The largest investments were in railroads and mining. The United States, of course, led the way, with over a billion dollars. The Fall Committee, based on the testimony of the witnesses that appeared before it, believed that Letcher had underestimated American investment by 50 percent. Whichever statistics one accepts, the American stake was enormous and crucial to the Mexican economy both before and after the Revolution.

From, "American, British, Mexican Investment in Mexico," in United States Senate, Committee on Foreign Relations, *Investigation of Mexican Affairs* (Washington, D.C.: Government Printing Office, 1920), 2:322–23.

The total wealth of Mexico as it appears in this table was $2,434,241,422, of which Americans owned $1,057,770,000; English, $321,302,800; and the Mexicans, $793,187,242. The figures given in the table as to British ownership should, from the best information in my possession, be increased from $321,000,000 to at least $800,000,000. The figures for American investment in mines should be increased very largely.

Mexican, largely in lands, town lots, etc. — Of the Mexican ownership over one-half was in lands, town lots, bank deposits, and bank stocks.

American investments are in tax-paying, labor-employing operations. — American investments in individual agriculture holdings are hereinafter set forth. The balance of the American investments was in railroads, mines, factories, oil, rubber, and property of this class, i.e., producing and labor-employing, tax-paying business — with the exception of about $50,000,000 in national bonds.

The Americans owned 78 per cent of the mines, 72 per cent of the smelters, 58 per cent of the oil, 68 per cent of the rubber business.

Railroads—American and English capital—Eighty-eight per cent are railroads. — The total railroad mileage was about 16,000 miles, in which American and English capital was invested (to extent about 88 per cent) and which their capitalists had constructed to that extent.

The . . . table shows only an investment of about $3,150,000 in ranches and about $13,000,000 in timberlands, farms, houses and lots, and personal property.

This statement is entirely incorrect as specific testimony before this committee shows that more than 3,000 American families of an average of five persons each owned their own homes either in colonies or in separate locations, all of whom were engaged in agriculture and that the actual average loss to such families has been approximately $10,000 each, or a total in this one item of $30,000,000, not taking into consideration the value of the land nor of the houses and other improvements which could not or have not been destroyed.

In this connection we are not considering the very large amounts invested in cattle ranches devoted purely to stock raising, nor in estimating this loss have we included the loss upon rubber, coffee, sugar, and other like large plantations.

Table 1. *Valuations*

CLASS.	AMERICAN.	ENGLISH.	FRENCH.	MEXICAN.	ALL OTHER.
Railway stocks	$235,464,000	$81,237,800	—	$125,440,000	$75,000
Railway bonds	408,926,000	87,680,000	$17,000,000	12,275,000	38,535,380
Bank stocks	7,850,000	5,000,000	31,000,000	31,950,000	3,250,000
Bank deposits	22,700,000	—	—	161,963,042	18,560,000
Mines	223,000,000	43,600,000	5,000,000	7,500,000	7,830,000
Smelters	26,500,000	—	—	7,200,000	3,000,000
National bonds	52,000,000	67,000,000	60,000,000	21,000,000	—
Timberlands	8,100,000	10,300,000	—	5,600,000	750,000
Ranches	3,150,000	2,700,000	—	14,000,000	—
Farms	960,000	760,000	—	47,000,000	1,250,000
Live stock	9,000,000	—	—	47,450,000	3,800,000
Houses and personal	4,500,000	680,000	—	127,020,000	2,760,000
Cotton mills	—	450,000	19,000,000	6,000,000	4,750,000
Soap factories	1,200,000	—	—	2,780,000	3,600,000
Tobacco factories	—	—	3,238,000	4,712,000	895,000
Breweries	600,000	—	178,000	2,822,000	1,250,000
Factories	9,600,000	2,780,000	—	3,270,200	3,000,000
Public utilities	760,000	8,000,000	—	5,155,000	275,000

Table 1. *Valuations* (continued)

CLASS.	AMERICAN.	ENGLISH.	FRENCH.	MEXICAN.	ALL OTHER.
Stores:					
Wholesale	$2,700,000	$110,000	$7,000,000	$2,800,000	$14,270,000
Retail	1,780,000	30,000	680,000	71,235,000	2,175,000
Oil business	15,000,000	10,000,000	—	650,000	—
Rubber industry	15,000,000	—	—	4,500,000	2,500,000
Professional	3,600,000	850,000	—	1,560,000	1,100,000
Insurance	4,000,000	—	—	2,000,000	3,500,000
Theaters	20,000	—	—	1,575,000	500,000
Hotels	260,000	—	—	1,730,000	710,000
Institutions	1,200,000	125,000	350,000	74,000,000	200,000
Total	1,057,770,000	321,302,800	143,446,000	792,187,242	118,535,380

NOTE. — From the testimony taken and other evidence in the possession of the committee, the committee reports that the total amount of American investments in Mexico in 1911 were more nearly $1,500,000,000 than the total set forth in the column above, $1,057,770,000.

39

THE UNITED STATES–MEXICAN COMMISSION

The Bucareli Agreements

1923

Article 27 of the Constitution of 1917 allocated all subsoil rights to the nation. The administrations of U.S. presidents Woodrow Wilson and Warren G. Harding withheld recognition of the government of elected president General Alvaro Obregón (1920–1924) because of this contro-versial provision. Foreign mining and petroleum companies feared the loss of their investments to expropriation. In May 1923, after five years of unfruitful negotiations, representatives of the two nations met in Mexico City at 85 Bucareli Street. The issues concerning subsoil rights claims made after 1917 were left unresolved, but the Mexican government reiter-ated that the provisions of Article 27 were not to be enforced retroactively as long as the holder of mineral or oil rights had performed prior posi-tive acts to obtain the underground resources. Although the Bucareli Agreements, signed in May, were subject to various interpretations, they allowed foreign companies to continue their operations and the United States to grant recognition to the Obregón government. The status of the petroleum companies remained contentious for the next fifteen years. In 1938, the Mexican government expropriated them, defying a Mexican Supreme Court ruling forcing them to raise the wages of their employees.

A meeting of the Conferences was held at 10 o'clock a.m., August 2, 1923, at No. 85 Bucareli Street. Present: American Commissioners Charles Beecher Warren and John Barton Payne; Mexican Commissioners Ramón Ross and Fernando González Roa.

The MEXICAN COMMISSIONERS stated that the following are natural consequences of the political and administrative program which the Mexican Government has been carrying out, and that they state them in behalf of their Government in connection with the representations

From United States–Mexican Commission, "Notes on Formal Meeting, August 2, 1923," in *Proceedings of the United States–Mexican Commission, Convened in Mexico City, May 14, 1923* (Washington, D.C.: Government Printing Office, 1925), 47–49.

relating to the rights of the citizens of the United States of America in respect to the subsoil.

I. It is the duty of the federal executive power, under the constitution, to respect and enforce the decisions of the judicial power. In accordance with such a duty, the Executive has respected and enforced, and will continue to do so, the principles of the decisions of the Supreme Court of Justice in the "Texas Oil Company" case and the four other similar . . . cases, declaring that paragraph IV of Article 27 of the Constitution of 1917 is not retroactive in respect to all persons who have performed, prior to the promulgation of said Constitution, some positive act which would manifest the intention of the owner of the surface or of the persons entitled to exercise his rights to the oil under the surface to make use of or obtain the oil under the surface: such as drilling, leasing, entering into any contract relative to the subsoil, making investments of capital in lands for the purpose of obtaining the oil in the subsoil, carrying out works of exploitation and exploration of the subsoil and in cases where from the contract relative to the subsoil it appears that the grantors fixed and received a price higher than would have been paid for the surface of the land because it was purchased for the purpose of looking for oil and exploiting same if found; and, in general, performing or doing any other positive act, or manifesting an intention of a character similar to those heretofore described. According to these decisions of the Supreme Court, the same rights enjoyed by those owners of the surface who have performed a positive act or manifested an intention such as has been mentioned above, will be enjoyed also by their legal assignees or those persons entitled to the rights to the oil. The protection of the Supreme Court extends to all the land or subsoil concerning which any of the above intentions have been manifested, or upon which any of the above specified acts have been performed, except in cases where the documents relating to the ownership of the surface or the use of the surface or the oil in the subsoil establish some limitation.

The above statement has constituted and will constitute in the future the policy of the Mexican Government, in respect to lands and the subsoil upon which or in relation to which any of the above-specified acts have been performed, or in relation to which any of the above specified intentions have been manifested; and the Mexican Government will grant to the owners, assignees or other persons entitled to the rights to the oil, drilling permits on such lands, subject only to police regulations, sanitary regulations and measures for public order and the right of the Mexican Government to levy general taxes.

II. The Government, from the time that these decisions of the Supreme Court were rendered, has recognized and will continue to recognize the same rights for all those owners or lessees of land or subsoil or other persons entitled to the rights to the oil who are in a similar situation as those who obtained *amparo*; that is, those owners or lessees of land or subsoil or other persons entitled to the rights to the oil who have performed any positive act of the character already described or manifested any intention such as above specified.

III. The Mexican Government, by virtue of the decisions of the President . . . dated January 17, 1920, and January 8, 1921, respectively, has granted and grants preferential rights to all owners of the surface or persons entitled to exercise their preferential rights to the oil in the subsoil, who have not performed a positive act such as already mentioned, showing their intention to use the subsoil or manifested an intention as above specified, so that whenever those owners of the surface or persons entitled to exercise their preferential rights to the oil in the subsoil wish to use or obtain the oil in the said subsoil, the Mexican Government will permit them to do so to the exclusion of any third party who has no title to the land or to the subsoil.

IV. The present Executive, in pursuance of the policy that has been followed up to the present time, as above stated, and within the limitations of his constitutional powers, considers it just to grant, and will continue in the future to grant, as in the past, to owners of the surface or persons entitled to exercise their preferential rights to the oil, who have not performed prior to the Constitution of 1917 any positive act such as mentioned above, or manifested an intention as above specified, a preferential right to the oil and permits to obtain the oil to the exclusion of any third party who has no title to the land or subsoil, in accordance with the terms of the legislation now in force as modified by the decisions of January 17, 1920, and January 8, 1921, already mentioned. The above statement in this paragraph of the policy of the present Executive is not intended to constitute an obligation for an unlimited time on the part of the Mexican Government to grant preferential rights to such owners of the surface or persons entitled to exercise their rights to the oil in the subsoil.

V. The AMERICAN COMMISSIONERS have stated in behalf of their Government that the Government of the United States now reserves, and reserves should diplomatic relations between the two countries be resumed, all the rights of the citizens of the United States in respect to the subsoil under the surface of lands in Mexico owned by citizens of the United States, or in which they have an interest in whatever form owned or held, under the laws and Constitution of Mexico in force prior to the promulgation of the new Constitution, May 1, 1917, and under the principles of international law and equity. The MEXICAN COMMISSIONERS, while sustaining the principles hereinbefore set forth in this statement but reserving the rights of the Mexican Government under its laws as to lands in connection with which no positive act of the character specified in this statement has been performed or in relation to which no intention of the character specified in this statement has been manifested, and its rights with reference thereto under the principles of international law, state in behalf of their Government that they recognize the right of the United States Government to make any reservation of or in behalf of the rights of its citizens.

At 2 o'clock p.m. the Commissioners adjourned until 10 o'clock a.m. the following day, August 3, 1923.

L. LANIER WINSLOW
Secretary

H. RALPH RINGE
Assistant Secretary

JOHN URQUIDA
Secretary

A Chronology of the Mexican Revolution (1810–1940)

1810 Grito de Dolores (Cry of Dolores) proclaims Mexican independence.

1810–1821 Mexico wins its independence from Spain.

1836 Northern province of Texas rebels and wins its independence.

1846–1848 United States provokes war with Mexico; Mexico loses half its territory.

1857–1860 Conservatives and Liberals fight War of the Reform.

1858–1872 Benito Juárez president.

1861 Great Britain, Spain, and France invade Mexico.

1862–1867 France conquers most of Mexico, despite Mexican victory at Puebla on May 5, 1862 (Cinco de Mayo).

1876 General Porfirio Díaz rebels against Sebastián Lerdo de Tejada and takes over as president.

1880 Díaz peacefully leaves presidency to comply with his Anti-Reelectionist platform.

1884 Díaz returns as president and is reelected in 1888, 1892, 1896, 1900, 1904, and 1910.

Construction completed on Mexican Central Railroad, connecting Mexico City and El Paso, Texas.

1892 Díaz defeats rebellions in northern states.

1906 Enrique and Ricardo Flores Magón found Partido Liberal Mexicano (Mexican Liberal party).

Miners strike at Cananea copper mines.

1907 Economic depression hits Mexico and United States.

1908	American journalist James Creelman interviews Porfirio Díaz.
1910	Francisco I. Madero campaigns for presidency, is imprisoned, and flees into exile.
	Madero issues Plan of San Luis Potosí.
1911	Rebels under Pascual Orozco take Ciudad Juárez, Díaz goes into exile, and Madero is elected president.
1912	Dissatisfied with his treatment by Madero, Orozco rebels.
1913	General Bernardo Reyes and Félix Díaz stage coup that results in Ten Tragic Days.
	General Victoriano Huerta betrays and overthrows Madero.
	Venustiano Carranza leads resistance to Huerta.
1914	U.S. military occupies Veracruz and Tampico.
	Constitutionalist forces, led by Carranza, defeat Huerta.
	Constitutionalists split into two factions, with Emiliano Zapata and Francisco Villa allied against Carranza.
	Carranza legalizes divorce.
1914–1918	First World War.
1915	General Alvaro Obregón defeats Villa after a series of battles in central Mexico.
	United States recognizes Carranza government.
1916	Villa raids Columbus, New Mexico, provoking United States to invade Mexico with forces led by John J. Pershing.
	First feminist congress meets in Yucatán.
1917	Constitutional convention in Querétaro produces new constitution.
	German government sends Zimmermann telegram to Mexican government.
1919	Zapata assassinated.
1920	Obregón overthrows Carranza and is elected president.
1923	Mexico and United States sign Bucareli Agreements.
1924–1928	Plutarco Elías Calles president.
1928	Obregón wins election to second term but is assassinated before taking office.
1934–1940	Lázaro Cárdenas president.

Questions for Consideration

1. Historians have called the Mexican Liberal party (PLM) a precursor to the Revolution. How did it preview the demands of later groups?
2. How could Porfirio Díaz, a brilliant political tactician, have blundered so badly in his interview with James Creelman?
3. What were the major grievances of the middle class against the Díaz regime?
4. Why do you think the workers on the henequen plantations did not rebel despite their wretched conditions?
5. How were the demands of the Liberals, Francisco I. Madero, and Emiliano Zapata different? Did they have any elements in common?
6. Do you think that Villa, Obregón, Caraveo, and Treviño exhibit the characteristics of successful generals?
7. How did the Mexican generals view their troops?
8. Why was Alvaro Obregón able to defeat Francisco "Pancho" Villa in 1915?
9. Why was the Revolution so bloody?
10. How trustworthy are the accounts of the generals?
11. How would you characterize the lives of the soldiers?
12. What were the roles of women in the armies of the various revolutionary factions?
13. Why were the lives of the soldiers and *soldaderas* so hard?
14. If you had been a Mexican revolutionary, would you have deserted? What would have kept you fighting?
15. What were the main problems of civilians during the Revolution?
16. Why did some people decide to leave Mexico?
17. Who endured the worst conditions — women, old people, or children?
18. Do you think Eduardo Iturbide did a good job administering the Federal District? Why or why not?
19. Do you think the Agrarian Law of January 6, 1915, was a true reflection of Venustiano Carranza's views on agrarian reform?

20. How does Martín Luis Guzmán characterize Carranza?

21. To what extent is Luis García Pimentel's assessment of the Revolution correct?

22. Women were at the forefront of civilian politics during the Revolution. What were their goals? Did they achieve them?

23. Did the peasants win the Revolution? Why or why not?

24. Were foreigners treated badly by the revolutionaries? Were they treated any differently than Mexicans?

25. What were the most controversial aspects of the Constitution of 1917 and why?

26. Did women derive any specific benefits from the Constitution of 1917?

27. Is Henry Lane Wilson's rendition of his role in the overthrow of Madero credible? Why or why not?

28. Why was the Zimmermann telegram so objectionable to the United States, and why did Carranza not accept the German offer?

29. Why did the United States take such a keen interest in the Revolution?

30. Why were subsoil rights so important?

31. Do you think U.S. diplomats understood Mexico?

Selected Bibliography

PRIMARY SOURCES

Bonfils Batalla, Guillermo. *Mi pueblo durante la Revolución*. 3 vols. Mexico City: Instituto Nacional de Antropología e Historia, 1988.
Bush, I. J. *Gringo Doctor*. Caldwell, Idaho: Caxton, 1939.
Evans, Rosalie. *The Rosalie Evans Letters from Mexico*. Indianapolis: Bobbs-Merrill, 1926.
Guzmán, Martín Luis. *Memoirs of Pancho Villa*. Translated by Virginia H. Taylor. Austin: University of Texas Press, 1965.
La Revolución Mexicana a traves de sus documentos. 4 vols. México Universidad Autónoma de México, 1987.
O'Shaughnessy, Edith. *Diplomatic Days*. New York: Harper and Brothers, 1917.
Reed, John. *Insurgent Mexico*. New York: Appleton, 1914.
Turner, John Kenneth. *Barbarous Mexico*. Chicago: Charles H. Kerr, 1910.
United States Senate. Committee on Foreign Relations. *Investigation of Mexican Affairs*. Vol. 2. Washington, D.C.: Government Printing Office, 1920.
Wilson, Henry Lane. *Diplomatic Episodes in Mexico, Belgium and Chile*. New York: Doubleday, Page, 1927.

SECONDARY SOURCES

Beezley, William H., and Colin M. MacLachlan. *Mexicans in Revolution, 1910–1946: An Introduction*. Lincoln: University of Nebraska Press, 2009.
Benjamin, Thomas, and Mark Wasserman, eds. *Provinces of the Revolution: Essays on Regional Mexican History, 1911–1929*. Albuquerque: University of New Mexico Press, 1990.
Blum, Ann S. *Domestic Economies: Family, Work, and Welfare in Mexico City, 1884–1943*. Lincoln: University of Nebraska Press, 2009.
Brenner, Anita. *The Wind That Swept Mexico: The History of the Mexican Revolution*. Austin: University of Texas Press, 1971.
Brunk, Samuel. *Emiliano Zapata: Revolution and Betrayal in Mexico*. Albuquerque: University of New Mexico Press, 1995.
Cumberland, Charles C. *Mexican Revolution: Genesis under Madero*. Austin: University of Texas Press, 1952.

————. *Mexican Revolution: The Constitutionalist Years.* Austin: University of Texas Press, 1972.

Fowler-Salamini, Heather, and Mary Kay Vaughan, eds. *Women in the Mexican Countryside, 1850–1990.* Tucson: University of Arizona Press, 1994.

Friedrich, Paul. *Agrarian Revolt in a Mexican Village.* Englewood Cliffs, N.J.: Prentice-Hall, 1970.

Gilly, Adolfo. *The Mexican Revolution.* New York: New Press, 2005.

Gonzales, Michael J. *The Mexican Revolution, 1910–1940.* Albuquerque: University of New Mexico Press, 2002.

Hall, Linda. *Alvaro Obregón: Power and Revolution in Mexico, 1911–1920.* College Station: Texas A&M Press, 1981.

Hart, John Mason. *Revolutionary Mexico: The Coming and Process of the Mexican Revolution.* Berkeley: University of California Press, 1987.

Joseph, Gilbert M. *Revolution from Without: Yucatán, Mexico, and the United States, 1880–1924.* Cambridge: Cambridge University Press, 1982.

Katz, Friedrich. *The Life and Times of Pancho Villa.* Stanford, Calif.: Stanford University Press, 1998.

————. *The Secret War in Mexico.* Chicago: University of Chicago Press, 1981.

Knight, Alan. *The Mexican Revolution.* 2 vols. Cambridge: Cambridge University Press, 1986.

Krauze, Enrique. *Biography of Power.* New York: HarperCollins, 1991.

LaFrance, David. *The Mexican Revolution in Puebla.* Wilmington, Del.: Scholarly Resources, 1989.

————. *Revolution in Mexico's Heartland: Politics, War, and State Building in Puebla, 1913–1920.* Wilmington, Del.: Scholarly Resources, 2003.

Lear, John. *Workers, Neighbors, and Citizens: The Revolution in Mexico City.* Lincoln: University of Nebraska Press, 2001.

Poniatowska, Elena. *Las Soldaderas: Women of the Mexican Revolution.* Translated by David Dorado Romo. El Paso, Tex.: Cinco Punto Press, 2006.

Porter, Susie S. *Working Women in Mexico City: Public Discourses and Material Conditions, 1870–1931.* Tucson: University of Arizona Press, 2003.

Quirk, Robert E. *An Affair of Honor: Woodrow Wilson and the Occupation of Veracruz.* New York: McGraw-Hill, 1962.

————. *The Mexican Revolution, 1914–1915: The Convention of Aguascalientes.* Bloomington: Indiana University Press, 1960.

Salas, Elizabeth. *Soldaderas in the Mexican Revolution: Myth and History.* Austin: University of Texas Press, 1990.

Smith, Robert Freeman. *The United States and Revolutionary Nationalism in Mexico, 1916–1923.* Chicago: University of Chicago Press, 1972.

Tuchman, Barbara W. *The Zimmerman Telegram.* New York: Macmillan, 1966.

Tutino, John. *From Insurrection to Revolution in Mexico: Social Bases of Agrarian Violence, 1750–1940.* Princeton, N.J.: Princeton University Press, 1986.

Wells, Allen, and Gilbert M. Joseph. *Summer of Discontent, Seasons of Upheaval*. Durham, N.C.: Duke University Press, 1996.

Womack, John, Jr. *Zapata and the Mexican Revolution*. New York: Knopf, 1969.

FICTION

Azuela, Mariano. *The Underdogs*. Translated by Frederick H. Fornoff. Prospect Heights, Ill. Waveland Press, 2002.

Fuentes, Carlos, *The Death of Artemio Cruz*. New York: Farrar, Straus and Giroux, 1964.

Guzmán, Martín Luis. *The Eagle and the Serpent*. Translated by Harriet de Onís. Garden City, N.Y.: Dolphin Books, 1965.

López y Fuentes, Gregorio. *El Indio*. Translated by Anita Brenner. New York: Bobbs-Merrill, 1937.

Traven, B. *The General from the Jungle*. New York: Hill and Wang, n.d.

———. *Government*. Chicago: Ivan R. Dee, 1993.

———. *The Rebellion of the Hanged*. Chicago: Ivan R. Dee, 1994.

Acknowledgments (*continued from p. iv*)

Document 5: From Francisco Villa, "Unpublished Memoir," excerpted in Friedrich Katz, *The Secret War in Mexico*. Copyright © 1981, University of Chicago Press. Reprinted by permission of Friedrich Katz.

Document 7: Excerpt from *Government* by B. Traven. Copyright © 1975 by B. Traven. Reprinted by permission of Hill and Wang, a division of Farrar, Straus and Giroux, LLC.

Document 8: José Guadalupe Posada, *Los sangrientos sucesos en la Ciudad de Puebla*. Zinc etching, 1910, 11-5/8 x 7-15/16 inches. Reprinted by permission, Amon Carter Museum of American Art, Fort Worth, Texas, 1978.115.

Document 11: From *Memoirs of Pancho Villa* by Martín Luis Guzmán, translated by Virginia H. Taylor, Copyright © 1965, renewed 1993. By permission of the University of Texas Press.

Document 12: From J. B. Treviño to Alvaro Obregón, dispatch, no date, in Friedrich Katz, "La ultima Gran Campaña de Francisco Villa," *Boletín*, no. 5. Copyright © 1991 Fideicomiso Archivos Plutarco Elías Calles y Fernando Torreblanca. Reprinted by permission of Fideicomiso Archivos Plutarco Elías Calles y Fernando Torreblanca.

Document 13: From Richard M. Estrada, "Zapata to Villa," *Proceedings of the Pacific Coast Council of Latin American Studies* 8. Copyright 1981. Reprinted by permission of the Pacific Coast Council on Latin American Studies.

Document 16: From Anthony Quinn, *The Original Sin: A Self-Portrait*. Copyright © 1972 Anthony Quinn. Reprinted by permission of the Anthony Quinn Foundation.

Document 17: From Esther R. Pérez, James Kallas, and Nina Kallas, eds., *Those Years of the Revolution, 1910–1920: Authentic Bilingual Life Experiences as Told by the Veterans of the War*. Copyright © 1974, Esther R. Pérez, James Kallas, and Nina Kallas. Reprinted by permission of Nina Kallas.

Document 18: Memorias del General de División Marcela Caraveo. MS193. C.L. Reprinted by permission, Sonnichsen Special Collections Dept., University of Texas at El Paso Library.

Document 19: Photo 1, *Zapatistas on March to Xochimilco*: © Bettmann/Corbis; Photo 2, *Villa*: courtesy of the Library of Congress, reproduced by permission of Brown Brothers.

Document 20: From Elizabeth Salas, *Soldaderas of the Mexican Military*. Copyright © 1990 University of Texas Press. Reprinted by permission of the University of Texas Press.

Document 21: Printed with Permission from the Continuum International Publishing Group. Gregorio López y Fuentes © 1937.

Document 23: Excerpt of letter from Edith Henry to her brother, spring 1916. Reprinted by permission of Julia Swanson.

Document 24: From Interview of Frank Galván by Mary Lee Nolan, March 14, 1973. Copyright © 1973, Cushing Library, Texas A & M University. Reprinted by permission of the Cushing Library, Texas A & M University.

Document 25: From *The Eagle and the Serpent* by Martín Luis Guzmán, translated by Harriet de Onis, translation copyright © 1965 by Doubleday, a division of Random House, Inc. Copyright 1930 by Alfred A. Knopf, Inc., a division of Random House, Inc. Used by permission of Doubleday, a division of Random House, Inc.

Document 30: Excerpt from speech of Francisca García Ortiz, January 13, 1916, in Alaide Foppa and Helene F. de Aguilar, "The First Feminist Congress in Mexico, 1916," in *Signs* 6:1, pp. 192–99. Copyright © 1979, University of Chicago Press. Reprinted by permission of University of Chicago Press.

Index

activism, by workers, 21
"Adelita" (*corrido*), 91
Administration of Intervened Property of
    Chihuahua, 20
"Agrarian Law, The" (Carranza), 109–11
agriculture
    Carranza's Agrarian Law and, 109–11
    damage by armies, 16
Aguascalientes, convention in (1914), 105
Aguirre Benavides, Eugenio, 60, 81
Allies (World War I), U.S. in, 25
Almeida, Antonio, 81
Alvarado, Salvador, and feminist congress in
    Yucatán, 117
Amaro, Joaquin, 67, 82
"American, British, and Mexican Investment
    in Mexico" (Letcher), 144–47
American Smelting and Refining Company,
    Mexican interests of, 24
Angeles, Felipe, 82, 107
annexation, of Texas by U.S., 3
Anti-Reelectionists, 7
    Díaz and, 152
Arango, Doroteo. *See* Villa, Francisco
    "Pancho"
Argúmendo, Benjamín, 81, 82
armies, in Revolution, 10, 13
arms and ammunition, 14
Article 27, of 1917 Constitution, 22, 25,
    121–25, 148
Article 123, of 1917 Constitution, 22, 126–28
assassinations
    of Madero, 11
    of Obregón, 153
    of Zapata, 12, 153
    See also specific individuals
autonomy, local and state, 3–4, 21
Avila, Fidel, 60, 61
Avila, Jesús, experiences of the war, 78,
    79–81
Azuela, Mariano, 51

Balderrama, Modesto, 79
bankruptcies, in economic depression of
    1907–1909, 4
banks, property loans by, 124
"Barbarous Mexico" (Turner), 40–46
barbed wire, as revolutionary defense, 15
"Battle at Celaya, The" (Obregón), 66–68
"Battle of Tierra Blanca, The" (Villa), 59–62
battles
    adaptation to shifting sides in, 16–17
    at Celaya, 15, 66–68
    at Ciudad Juárez, 9, 15, 153
    at Gomez Palacio, 52, 54
    at León, 15
    of Tierra Blanca, 52, 59–62
    See also specific battles
"Bloody Dawn, The" (Reed), 53, 54–58
"Bloody Events in the City of Puebla, The"
    (Posada), 48–49, 49f
Bonfil Batalla, Guillermo, "My Village dur-
    ing the Revolution," 94–96
Brenner, Anita, and George Leighton, "Pho-
    tographs of Soldiers and Soldaderas,"
    86, 87f, 88f, 89f, 90f
Britain. *See* England (Britain)
Bucareli Agreements, 25, 153
"Bucareli Agreements, The" (United States–
    Mexican Commission), 148–51
bureaucracy, after Díaz, 10

Cabrera, Miguel, 48–49, 49f
caciques, 38, 39
Caden, Rosalie. *See* Evans, Rosalie
Calles, Plutarco Elías, 8, 26, 153
Camara de Agricola (planters organization),
    44n
Camara Zavala, Enrique, 43
Cananea copper mines, strike at, 6, 152
Canton, Felipe G., 44
Caraveo, Marcelo, 60
    "Fighting without Pay," 85

161